Prayers

of

Blessing

Over Your

Husband

Bruce Wilkinson

Heather Hair

HARVEST HOUSE PUBLISHERS
EUGENE, OREGON

Unless otherwise indicated, all Scripture quotations are from the Holy Bible, New International Version®, NIV®. Copyright © 1973, 1978, 1984, 2011 by Biblica, Inc.® Used by permission. All rights reserved worldwide.

Verses marked NKJV are taken from the New King James Version®. Copyright © 1982 by Thomas Nelson, Inc. Used by permission. All rights reserved.

Verses marked NASB are taken from the New American Standard Bible®, © 1960, 1962, 1963, 1968, 1971, 1972, 1973, 1975, 1977, 1995 by The Lockman Foundation. Used by permission. (www.Lockman.org)

Verses marked ESV are from The ESV® Bible (The Holy Bible, English Standard Version®), copyright © 2001 by Crossway, a publishing ministry of Good News Publishers. Used by permission. All rights reserved.

Cover by Rightly Designed, Buckley, Washington

Author photos by Dylan and Tayte Gerik

PRAYERS OF BLESSING OVER YOUR HUSBAND
Copyright © 2018 Bruce Wilkinson and Heather Hair
Published by Harvest House Publishers
Eugene, Oregon 97408
www.harvesthousepublishers.com

ISBN: 978-0-7369-7181-2 (pbk.)
ISBN: 978-0-7369-7182-9 (eBook)

Library of Congress Cataloging-in-Publication Data

Names: Wilkinson, Bruce, author.
Title: Prayers of blessing over your husband / Bruce Wilkinson and Heather Hair.
Description: Eugene, Oregon : Harvest House Publishers, 2018.
Identifiers: LCCN 2017046611 (print) | LCCN 2018003708 (ebook) | ISBN 9780736971829 (ebook) | ISBN 9780736971812 (pbk.)
Subjects: LCSH: Wives—Prayers and devotions.
Classification: LCC BV4528.15 (ebook) | LCC BV4528.15 .W54 2018 (print) | DDC 242/.8435—dc23
LC record available at https://lccn.loc.gov/2017046611

Printed in the United States of America

19 20 21 22 23 24 25 26 / VP-SK / 10 9 8 7 6 5 4

This book is dedicated to all the wives who seek the best for their husbands through their prayers, love, and support. May you find great encouragement and many helpful insights that will enable your prayers to receive an abundance of blessings from the Lord for your husband.

As this book was written, I found myself repeatedly thanking the Lord for my faithful and praying wife, Darlene, as she is the best illustration I know of everything Heather and I wrote about. The impact of her prayers, support, encouragement, and love cannot be overestimated.

Through hundreds of her prayers over the decades of our marriage, I, as her husband, have been able to serve the Lord far beyond anything either of us could ever have dreamed possible. She has continued pursuing the Lord in ever-increasing diligence and, because of that, we have experienced an amazing life together.

I would be the first to publicly recognize her as a godly woman of whom I have often quoted this passage from Proverbs 31 as coming true in her life: *"Her children rise up and bless her; her husband also, and he praises her, saying: 'Many daughters have done nobly, but you excel them all'"* (verses 28-29 NASB).

Contents

Part 1: The Mantle of a Wife's Prayer

Chapter One: Your Mantle 11

Chapter Two: The Power of Your Mantle 17

Chapter Three: The Mantle of Heaven's Helper 25

Chapter Four: Five Secrets to Maximize Your Mantle 33

Chapter Five: Using Your Mantle Effectively 43

Part 2: Taking On the Mantle of Prayer

1. Character: Love 53

2. Character: Joy 55

3. Character: Peace 57

4. Character: Forbearance 59

5. Character: Kindness 61

6. Character: Goodness 63

7. Character: Faithfulness 65

8. Character: Gentleness 67

9. Character: Self-Control 69

10. Courage: Waging Spiritual Warfare 71

11. Courage: Overcoming Challenges 73

12. Conflict: The Power of Truth, Righteousness,
    and Peace 75

13. Conflict: Tools of Faith and Trust 77

14. Conflict: Using the Word of God 79

15. Conflict: Power of Prayer 81

16. Character: Love God and Trust Him
      to Supply Your Needs 83

17. Courage: Teachable Spirit 85

18. Community: Ministry Opportunities
      in the Church or Community 87

19. Courage: Stir Up the Dream Within Him 89

20. Career: Flourish and Enjoy His Work 91

21. Character: Protection from Immoral
      Relationships and Pornography 93

22. Career: Traveling Mercies 95

23. Career: Eternal Perspective 97

24. Career: Favor on the Job 99

25. Communication: Listening to God's Guidance 101

26. Courage: Spiritual Leader of the Home 103

27. Character: Financial Stewardship 107

28. Communication: Handling Disagreements 109

29. Communion: Reading and Meditating on
      God's Word 111

30. Communion: Abiding Relationship with Christ 113

31. Confession: Repenting of Sins 115

32. Communion: Having the Mind of Christ 117

33. Community: Godly Male Friends and Mentors 119

34. Career: Protection Physically, Emotionally,
      and Spiritually 121

35. Courage: Increase His Faith 123

36. Courage: Pure Heart 125

37. Courage: Facing Problems and Challenges 127

38. Character: Loyalty 129

39. Character: Direct His Attention to You and
    Away from Inappropriate Entertainment 131

40. Character: Taking Every Thought Captive 133

41. Courage: Cultivating Certainty 135

42. Commitment: Enriching Our Sexuality 137

43. Communion: Clarity on Direction 141

44. Communication: Supporting My Growth
    and Purpose 143

45. Community: Encouraging Other Couples 145

46. Communication: Talking with Each Other 147

47. Commitment: Physical Health 149

48. Commitment: Fun and Enjoyment 151

49. Character: Mutual Respect and Honor 153

50. Commitment: Accepting and Embracing Each Other 155

Part 1

The Mantle of
a Wife's Prayer

Chapter One

Your Mantle

I am delighted you picked up *Prayers of Blessing over Your Husband*. This reflects your desire to learn how to more positively impact your husband and your marriage! As you read through this book and then use the prayers on a regular basis, your husband is going to be one happy and even transformed man!

Prayer changes things, and as you will discover in this book, your prayers will bring about some major and encouraging changes in your husband. The Bible conveys the surprising fact that a wife's prayers for her husband are among the most powerful agents for change that exist anywhere. You may be pleasantly shocked to discover how powerful your prayers are and how carefully God pays attention to them.

If you truly long for God's miraculous intervention in your marriage, then embrace the fact that you wear an invisible but mighty covering I call the "Wife's Mantle." A mantle is defined by different dictionaries as "something that covers or surrounds; an important role or responsibility that passes from one person to another; a position of someone who has responsibility or authority." One dictionary gives an illustration of the use of the word *mantle* with this sentence: "She accepted the mantle of leadership."

The moment you walked that proverbial aisle and said "I do," God placed a mantle on you of responsibility and authority within the marriage bond, perhaps without you even being aware of it. Until that moment, you did not have the Wife's Mantle. You had the role of a daughter, perhaps the role of a sister, an employee, etc. But when you became a married woman, you took on a new role.

Unless you have been married before, your marriage vows launched a new and never-before-experienced role in your life.

If you don't understand how God established the wife's role in marriage, you may never enjoy true victory and happiness within your marriage because of either "role reversal" or "role abdication." Role reversal occurs in a marriage when the wife assumes the role of her husband, and role abdication occurs when the wife fails to fulfill her God-given responsibility or duty within the marriage.

As I helped innumerable couples and individual husbands and wives over the years, I discovered that very few people understand the importance of roles, especially within marriage.

In different circumstances, we all play different roles; that is, we act in certain ways in certain situations. Early in our marriage, I caused some problems because I forgot to change roles! I would come home from work with much on my mind and forget to change roles from president of an organization to husband of my wife. I can remember Darlene quipping, "Are you still at the office?" and "Am I your secretary?" which meant I forgot to come home and assume the "marriage role" as her loving husband.

After a few times of coming home in the wrong role, I invented a solution: I selected a certain restaurant that I always passed while driving home where I changed from my "business role" to my "husband role" and later added my "father role." Now, it was just as important that I flip back on my way to work. Just imagine if I neglected to switch on my way to work and came into the office relating to my assistant in my husband's role!

You can either invent your own role in marriage from movies and TV or continue to pattern your role after the way your mother fulfilled her role in marriage. But if you understand God's purposes for marriage and are wise, you can take a better path and discover the way God has established the wife's role and then pursue fulfilling it to the best of your ability. The comforting truth about embracing God's delegated role is that His position works for all marriages, at all times, regardless of your culture, your upbringing, or your husband's or your personality or abilities.

If I asked you to explain God's revealed truth about how He wants every wife to fulfill their role in marriage, what would you say?

Before moving any further on this topic, we need to understand that roles do not relate to importance or significance. Roles do not define you; they only are necessary within certain situations. For instance, when you are at work, you are not fulfilling your role as wife. I knew one couple in which the wife was the CEO of a big company and her husband was a salesperson at that company. In her role as CEO, she clearly could tell her employed husband what to do—and the husband had no authority over her but had to submit to her as CEO. But when that CEO and salesman drove home, they had to change roles from CEO and salesman to wife and husband. Very, very different. Married women are only to assume their married role with their husband when they are fulfilling their responsibilities within their marriage.

In Genesis 1–3, the Bible reveals that God invented marriage and established the key role for the wife in that relationship. God stated in Genesis 2:18 that His perfect creation needed one more act of creation to be complete because "it is not good for the man to be alone." At that point, God described the specific solution to that "not good" condition and said, "I will make a helper suitable for him." ("I will make him a helper comparable to him" [NKJV]; "I will make him a helper fit for him" [ESV]).

The Hebrew word translated "helper" is *ezer* and means "helper, one who aids." I've studied every time in the Bible that this word is used and it always simply means "to help," nothing more and nothing less. *Ezer* is used twice in Psalm 121:1-2: "I will lift up my eyes to the hills—from whence comes my *help*? My *help* comes from the LORD, who made heaven and earth" (NKJV, emphasis added).

When God solved the "aloneness" of Adam, He could have described the new person in all kinds of ways, but He specifically chose the word *helper*. God sovereignly formed another human in His image and likeness with the same instructions to "have dominion" over creation—but in regard to her husband, she was to be his helper.

The primary role of the wife in marriage (not outside of marriage or in any other role she may have in the marketplace or with other males) is to help her husband, to assist him, to aid him, to help him become and achieve more than he could ever become or do without her.

The Wife's Mantle is the sovereignly delegated role of assisting her husband to fulfill his calling. A wife can assist her husband in all kinds of ways, including with her actions and attitudes, and in this book, we are highlighting a third major tool she can use to assist him: her prayers.

As you read earlier, the Wife's Mantle carries God's delegated authority and responsibility to help her husband. This point cannot be emphasized enough, because it reveals how God feels when a wife prays for her husband. Her prayers to help her husband are in the very center of God's will! Not only is God pleased, but He responds to her with His help.

Chapter Two

The Power of Your Mantle

Y ou are the only helper God supernaturally and sovereignly assigned to the good of your husband.

Only you. No other human in the universe but you.

God reveals across the pages of the Holy Writ how He established universal roles, responsibilities, and rules governing everyone's marriage. God also sovereignly bestowed an indescribable power for the wife so she can excel as her husband's helper beyond the ordinary. Why? Because God delegated to you the power necessary to maximize the life of your husband beyond his and your imagination.

How true is the quip "Behind every successful man is an even greater woman"! Now, after almost 50 years of marriage, I've been asked to reveal to you my wife's secrets. Not just secrets she knows, but secrets she has used "on me for me" for decades. And, as the recipient of her anointed Mantle as my precious and treasured wife, I cannot find adequate words to express how she has connected with heaven and transformed her husband, for Christ's glory and for both of our benefits.

Thankfully, I have discovered the "Husband's Mantle" and used it for decades, but that's another book, isn't it? The Bible states that I am to be the "head" of my wife for her personal benefit (Ephesians 5:23). Just like Jesus in His headship over the church, I am to lead her so that Ephesians 5:27 becomes true about her: "That He might present her to Himself a glorious church, not having spot or wrinkle or any such thing, but that she should be holy and without blemish" (NKJV). Who the wife becomes is not only the responsibility of the wife, but equally, and even perhaps more surprisingly, lies on the shoulders of the mantled husband. Marriage is created to be a two-way transformational path: As the wife helps the husband to become more like Christ, so the husband leads the wife to become more like Christ.

Life comes packaged with struggles, failures, sins, betrayals, hurts, wounds, disappointments, and crushing defeats. Marriage provides the overcoming power not only to endure but to learn and eventually overcome by the grace of God.

Our marriage has experienced all such challenges—one cannot live as long as we have without undergoing all the normal temptations, misunderstandings, and failures—yet today we stand together, stronger than ever and more in love than when we walked down that glittering path on our wedding day.

If you think you'll be able to avoid experiencing similar difficulties in your marriage, you are naïve, as you will experience disappointments, discouragement, and despair. Why? Because your expectations are not realistic in this fallen world. All of us struggle with our selfish sin-nature that must be brought into submission to the Holy Spirit and the Scriptures.

Our response to the challenges life brings is always more important than the actual event. As Jesus and others in the Bible said so many times, the point of life is to "overcome" that which is difficult and painful. Each of those difficult moments or seasons is simply an obstacle that God permitted in your life so you can learn the deeper secrets of how to overcome and enjoy surpassing victories. They are actually gifts that feel like problems but are heaven's hidden stepping-stones to becoming more like

Christ, who overcame everything thrown against Him. Indeed, said He, "I have [even] overcome the world" (John 16:33 NKJV).

The Wife's Mantle is the powerful tool that enables you to unlock everything and anything so that you can overcome as a wife, secretly bringing your husband along with you in the process. What and who your husband becomes and achieves is massively related to the degree to which you have helped him. And wives who flourish in their role will inevitably hear this type of statement from their husband and children from Proverbs 31:28-29: "Her children rise up and call her blessed; her husband also, and he praises her: 'Many daughters have done well, but you excel them all'" (NKJV).

So before revealing the five universal secrets behind the Wife's Mantle, may I ask you a few questions, just to help you identify our starting point as it relates to you as your husband's helper?

1. Who has your husband become in his character because you have helped him?

2. What meaningful achievements has your husband enjoyed in his career because you helped him?

3. What are three specific desires that your husband has at this time that you are helping him achieve?

4. What are a couple of major weaknesses that you have had to bear with in your husband that slowly have disappeared because of your help?

If you are like most wives, you might have felt a bit uncomfortable in asking yourself those four questions. Why? Maybe because you never understood how deeply God desires you to follow His divine plan and help your husband.

I remember the day I asked Darlene how she felt she was

helping me as her husband. The question had never been discussed in the early years of our marriage. I think she may have taken a little offense as the answer should have been so obvious to me! "In a million ways, from cooking your meals, cleaning the house, washing your clothes, taking care of the children while you are at work and on trips…"

I nodded in full agreement, but then made a risky decision and asked her the following question: "Could I hire someone to clean the house, wash the dishes (hold on for a moment, I'm going somewhere!), even take care of the children?" She stepped back, her face projecting that this line of questioning was not going over so well.

I affirmed all the ways she helped me, but then asked the deeper question: "Do you think that all these necessary things make me feel helped?" She laughed and said, "They better have!" Then I flipped the focus and asked her, "Do you feel loved and helped by me when I work hard all week for you and the kids?" and "Do you really feel loved when I bring home my paycheck twice a month?" Ah, the expression on her face told me that a different perspective was starting to sink in.

Darlene then turned the question right back at me and asked, "Well, what do I do that makes you feel helped?" (And if this book was written to the husbands, then the question would be: "What do you do for your wife that makes her feel loved, special, and treasured?")

What would your husband's answer be if you asked him that question? That question became the stimulus for quite a number of very helpful and transforming conversations over the years of our marriage.

I told Darlene that to the degree she enjoyed and felt my love and affection and kindness was the degree to which I was succeeding in my role as her husband. In the same way, to the *degree I felt helped* in my own life was the degree to which she was succeeding at truly helping me.

With that in mind, you can better interpret and see the value of those four earlier questions. Go back and reread them and you'll see how thinking in this new direction can radically reframe how you think about fulfilling your role as your husband's helper.

Before moving on, we'd better stop for a minute and clear up a major misunderstanding that stops too many wives from ever really using their powerful Mantle.

Are you ready for a fuller understanding of your role? Take a deep breath and consider this statement:

> "The wife helps her husband regardless of his character, conduct, or attitudes."

Too often, wives think that their husbands must earn the right for them to help them. They will say, "If he is mean, or unloving, or selfish, why should I help him? He doesn't deserve it!"

You are absolutely right, he doesn't often deserve it! But could that be the wrong way of thinking?

God assigns the role of helper to the wife without any requirement on the part of the husband. In other words, a wife is to help her husband independent of his attitudes or actions.

It's exactly the same as what the Bible commands husbands: "Love your wives" (Ephesians 5:25). If you read all the verses in the Bible about that topic (I've studied every single one of them), you'll soon discover that there are no conditions or exceptions to a husband loving his wife either! She can be selfish, angry, nasty, and irresponsible—and yet the command remains: "Husbands, love your wives."

This is a very powerful principle, and implementing it can

be a major turning point in anyone's marriage. For the husband, it's unconditional love; for the wife, it's unconditional helping (two other commands are given as well, but they are outside of our present discussion). Husbands, therefore, are to love unconditionally, no matter what the wife may be doing at the time; likewise the wife.

God holds both husbands and wives accountable to obey Him in their marital roles, regardless of the behavior or response of their spouse. Since these directives are unconditional, then "helping" is not to be earned by good behavior, and "helping" cannot be forfeited by inappropriate behavior.

The Bible states this principle of the wife always seeking the benefit of her husband in Proverbs 31:11-12:

> The heart of her husband safely trusts her;
> So he will have no lack of gain.
> She does him good and not evil
> All the days of her life (NKJV).

"Doing him good" describes the intentional positive actions of the wife on behalf of her husband. "Not doing evil" describes the intentional lack of negative action of the wife toward her husband, regardless of his selfishness. Do you find any exceptions to either actions in these verses or anywhere else in the 1,189 chapters and 31,173 verses in the Bible, like "if he deserves it" or "when he obeys God"? You already know the answer. Not one exception. Never. Truly loving (for the husband to the wife) and helping (for the wife to the husband) is absolutely and always unconditional.

So, what's the result in the life of the husband whose wife fulfills the biblical role of helper in marriage? I'll never forget the day when I unexpectedly heard the answer to that question. During a weekend marriage retreat where Darlene and I were speaking, a woman came up to me at the break and said, "Do you want to know the result of being a godly helper? Look right in the middle of Proverbs 31 and read verse 23 and you'll find God's answer! It's the climax: When a wife fulfills her role as the husband's helper, then the husband becomes respected and even famous!" She smiled and then waited patiently for me to find it in my Bible.

As you can imagine, I couldn't wait to read verse 23, because I had no idea what she was referring to until I read the verse out loud:

> Her husband is known in the gates,
> When he sits among the elders of the land (NKJV).

She continued excitedly, "The most honored position in the Old Testament was to be invited to sit among the elders at the central city gate to dispense wisdom and direction for those who dwelled within that city. When a married woman truly embraces her God-given role within marriage," she said, "her man is going to become far more than he ever could by himself. He'll become respected in the community for his character and what he has achieved in life."

She once again smiled, and as she walked away said, "My man sits at the city gates because of my help. He couldn't help but become an elder in the land with me as his helper!"

So, how do I know what kind of husband I am? Just spend some time with my glorious wife. How does Darlene know what kind of wife she is? Just spend some time with her husband—and hopefully look for the nearby gates.

So, what's the power of the Wife's Mantle? Let's open the city gates and find out!

Chapter Three

The Mantle of Heaven's Helper

With God's clear purpose of "helping her husband to fulfill his God-given destiny with excellence" in mind, just think how heaven appreciates the wife who continually seeks to achieve that purpose! God's formula couldn't be any clearer, could it? God gave you to your husband as a gift to assist him in achieving the goals He has for him.

Wives are God's human partner to help mature and maximize their husband.

Now you know why God's ears are particularly open to the wife who prays for her husband! When a wife who "seeks to do her husband good" comes to the throne of the Almighty and asks for something to better help her husband, what do you think God's likely answer will be? She's fulfilling her calling in the very process of praying for God's help. She wants help to help. And God will grant that request.

When you reflect on the various ways the wife can support her husband from Proverbs 31, three primary methods surface:

1. Her consistent *actions* of doing "good" all the days of his life.

2. Her supportive *attitudes* and encouragement so that "her husband safely trusts her."

3. Her prayerful *appeals* to God on his behalf "so he will have no lack of gain."

Of everything that the Wife's Mantle carries, the power of your prayers goes beyond normal actions and attitudes. Why? Because your prayers appeal to God to supernaturally intervene in your husband's life. Your prayers are far more powerful than any action you may take or attitude you may demonstrate.

The wives who understand that God is more than willing to intervene in their husband's life due to their prayers inevitably see amazing results. Why? Because when your motives align with the role of helper that God established, then God is not only pleased, but He begins to put things into action in your husband's life that achieve both your and His will. And over time, your husband will likely become more and more the man of your dreams.

I'll never forget learning firsthand the amazing power of my wife's prayers for me in the early days of our marriage. Back then, I misunderstood how to be the "head" of our marriage with grace and kindness. One day a major decision had to be made, and although Darlene did her best to share her wisdom and change my mind, I didn't have ears to hear her.

After she saw I had made up my mind, she accepted the decision, even though she strongly disagreed. About a week later, I learned some new information that radically altered my decision. Over dinner I shared the fact that I had been wrong and had changed my mind.

She smiled but didn't say a word. When I asked her why she was smiling, she reluctantly revealed the reason. "Well, I knew your decision wasn't the right one and was going to negatively affect us and our family, but you just couldn't see it. I felt you would suffer in the future too. So I stopped arguing and just went over your head."

"Over my head?" I asked, kind of in shock.

She kindly responded, "Well, I couldn't help you, so I went directly to God and asked Him to change your mind for me."

I shook my head in disbelief, threw back my head, and laughed and laughed, and said, "Wow, what a great idea! Thanks for doing that, because I was definitely heading in the wrong direction and my decision would have been disastrous!"

Then it hit me. "So…how many times have you gone over my head?"

She smiled as only a wife can and replied, "I'll never tell! God seems to enjoy saying yes when I ask Him for help, and I'm thrilled that He does!"

"No kidding," I mumbled, feeling rather helpless.

In our conversations over the years, we have talked about this powerful prayer option available to all married women. One day she said rather pensively, "I had to learn that sometimes God didn't answer my prayer with a 'yes' but wanted you to learn from your mistakes the hard way. I came to realize that His answer was always the best one in the long-term for you and for me. Sometimes, though, I had to suffer from your mistakes, which was God's plan for me as well." My goodness, did I ever marry a priceless helper, way above my pay scale.

Thankfully, over the years I came to understand that God gave Darlene to me for balance and wisdom and safety. Because of that understanding, I cannot remember any major decision that we have not shared together—and it's been over 30 years since I made a big decision not to go forward (or backward) without her buy-in. Both of our lives are so much better because of my honoring her role as my God-given helper. But I never know when she may have already gone over my head in the process!

Before sharing the secrets of maximizing your Mantle as it

relates to your appeals to God on behalf of your husband, there is an exception to the power of your prayers in 1 Peter 3:7: "Husbands, likewise, dwell with them with understanding, giving honor to the wife, as to the weaker vessel, and as being heirs together of the grace of life, that your prayers may not be hindered" (NKJV). This sober warning—"that your prayers may not be hindered"—indicates that your husband's treatment of you can negatively affect how many "yeses" and "nos" you experience from your prayers.

If the husband is not loving his wife well, then he is breaking the primary command to husbands to "love your wives." Because the husband rebels against God's command and doesn't exercise understanding and give honor to his wife, then God disciplines his prayers and starts closing the doors of heaven to his requests. They bounce off the ceiling, and God turns a deaf ear to his prayers.

Unfortunately, however, God also hinders the effectiveness of the wife's prayers based upon the unloving actions and disobedience of the husband. How do we know that? Because 1 Peter 3:7 clearly states, "That your prayer may not be hindered" (NKJV). One might assume that the "your" refers solely to the prayers of a disobedient husband, but the Greek word translated "your" is not singular but plural—meaning the prayers of both the husband and the wife. This incentivizes the wife, who cannot control the negative behavior of her husband, to do everything in her power to help him treat her with kindness and respect.

What, then, should a wife do if her husband does not treat her with "understanding and giving honor"? The shocking answer is found in the preceding six verses of 1 Peter 3:1-6:

> Wives, likewise, be submissive to your own husbands, that even if some do not obey the word, they,

without a word, may be won by the conduct of their wives, when they observe your chaste conduct accompanied by fear. Do not let your adornment be merely outward—arranging the hair, wearing gold, or putting on fine apparel—rather let it be the hidden person of the heart, with the incorruptible beauty of a gentle and quiet spirit, which is very precious in the sight of God. For in this manner, in former times, the holy women who trusted in God also adorned themselves, being submissive to their own husbands, as Sarah obeyed Abraham, calling him lord, whose daughters you are if you do good and are not afraid with any terror (NKJV).

Often when a husband withholds understanding and honor from his wife, she is blatantly disobeying God's instructions in her role as his wife. If you need a major change in your marriage and more "yesses" in your prayers, then see how you are doing according to 1 Peter 3:1-6.

———

Before sharing how you can maximize your Mantle, I would like to conclude with a few words spoken from my heart to your heart. Whenever someone hears the word *helper* today, wouldn't you agree that it often brings up negative emotions, perhaps even with a touch of a despising attitude. Who looks up to, respects, or wants to be a helper?

When I began studying what the Bible teaches about marriage, I studied every verse on the topic, including the key Hebrew and Greek words behind our English translations. *Helper* is obviously one of the key marriage words, so I traced the original Hebrew word behind *helper* in every verse in the

Old Testament. What I learned radically changed my attitudes about the helper from a negative to a shining positive. Let me explain.

Your overall attitude about being the "helper" controls your attitude and therefore your actions. If you despise a role, then you certainly won't put much effort into fulfilling it, nor gain much joy from it, because you won't think very highly about it.

So, who does the Bible refer to as "helper" and is seen more than anyone else as the one who helps?

The answer is God Himself. Over and over again you find God helping others, coming to their rescue, providing what they need, protecting them. Now think about that for a moment. To help is to be like God! How about that paradigm shift, from despising the concept of helper to embracing it as godly?

In the Old Testament, God the Father is directly involved in helping and serving many different people. David stated it this way in Psalm 54:4: "Behold, God is my helper" (NKJV).

In the Gospels, God the Son is always serving (another word related to helping) other people. In fact, Jesus said that He was sent by the Father to serve others and to sacrifice Himself for our sins—giving His life to help others with their sin problem. Jesus referred to Himself as a "Helper" in John 14:16: "And I will pray the Father, and He will give you *another* Helper, that He may abide with you forever" (NKJV, emphasis added).

In the New Testament epistles, the Holy Spirit is given to us to be our Helper in John 14:26: "But the Helper, the Holy Spirit, whom the Father will send in My name, He will teach you all things, and bring to your remembrance all things that I said to you" (NKJV). Also in John 16:7: "Nevertheless I tell you the truth. It is to your advantage that I go away; for if I do not go away, the Helper will not come to you; but if I depart, I will send Him to you" (NKJV).

And one of the most straightforward revelations about how we are to think about the role of helper is in Hebrews 13:6: "So we may boldly say: 'The LORD is my helper; I will not fear. What can man do to me?'" (NKJV).

Examining all these passages caused me to totally reevaluate my attitudes toward the concept of "helper." I realized that to be like God, I must be a servant and help others. Jesus even stated that the greatest among us will be servants of all (Matthew 23:11).

Will you then change your mind and heart about your God-given role in marriage and embrace the nobility and God-like nature of serving as your husband's helper? Always keep in mind that you don't help your husband because he deserves it, but because it's the Lord's will for you!

Open your heart right now, and if you need to, ask the Lord to forgive your past misunderstanding and lack of wholehearted helping of your husband. Embrace fully the Lord's call on your life with your Mantle shining brightly!

Become even more godly than you are at this moment, because you chose to run toward the role of helper as God runs toward you to help you succeed.

There is one last passage of the Bible that surprisingly reveals how God helps people help others from the life of King David in 1 Chronicles 12:18:

> Then the Spirit came upon Amasai, chief of the captains, and he said:
>
> "We are yours, O David;
> We are on your side, O son of Jesse!
> Peace, peace to you,
> And peace to your helpers!
> For your God helps you."

So David received them, and made them captains
of the troop (NKJV).

When you rejoice and thank God for your godly role, then
heaven will rejoice and your husband won't know what hit him!

Now you are ready to learn and apply the five secrets of how
to become a Master Helper in your prayer life for your husband.

Chapter Four

Five Secrets to Maximize Your Mantle

Whenever a wife awakens to the will of God as revealed in His Word regarding her role as the helper to her husband, she begins asking very different questions than before. Instead of "Why isn't he…," she now muses, "How can I maximize my positive impact on my husband so that God will be pleased by my assistance?"

Keep in mind that the Bible is clear that the primary difference between the husband and wife is found in their distinctive roles. Man and woman, husband and wife—God created both equally in His own image as seen in Genesis 1:27: "So God created man in His own image; in the image of God He created him; male and female He created them" (NKJV).

Second, God gave identical responsibilities to the man as husband and woman as wife in Genesis 1:28: "Then God blessed them, and God said to them, 'Be fruitful and multiply; fill the earth and subdue it; have dominion over the fish of the sea, over the birds of the air, and over every living thing that moves on the earth'" (NKJV).

What is critical to remember, then, is husband and wife are equally made in the image and likeness of God and were equally delegated the dominion over the earth. Beyond that, the distinctive roles each are to fulfill are God's sovereign decision. For the wife, her role is to help the husband in fulfilling God's dreams for them both.

In this chapter, I would like to explore five secrets that will maximize the power of your Mantle, specifically focused on your prayerful appeals to God on your husband's behalf.

As you read through the 50 prayers included in part two to help you help him, you'll immediately recognize that most of the prayers fit into one of the five primary secrets outlined below. Guiding these secrets are three key people who must always be kept foremost in your mind:

1. God: How can I help my husband to the pleasure and glory of God?

2. Husband: How can I help my husband to his pleasure and benefit?

3. Wife: How can I help my husband so that our family is filled with fulfillment and joy?

Secret #1: Appeal to God in prayer to help your husband succeed in his work.

God wired men to achieve and to labor to become successful in their work. Not that women don't desire to achieve and become successful in their work, but this book's primary focus is on the role of the wife to help her husband in his work in the marketplace, in addition to her work at home, church, neighborhood, family, and in the marketplace.

For a few years, I served as one of the keynote speakers for a national ministry, speaking to stadiums jammed full of 40,000, 50,000, 60,000, and even 80,000 men. Men deeply long to succeed in their work; in fact, if a man continues to fail in his work, he will probably struggle in every other area of his life. Therefore, help him succeed by appealing to heaven for supernatural help in his work and ask these kinds of questions from time to time:

- Ask your husband what's the biggest breakthrough he wishes he could have this week.

- If he has a big sales presentation, ask him for the size of the order he's hoping to achieve.

- When he is seeking to hire another employee, ask him what kind of person he is looking for.

- Ask him if he would like a major promotion and, if he does, what needs to happen to achieve it.

In other words, ask your husband questions that will reveal the specific ways you can appeal to God on his behalf. Don't just ask God to "please help my husband at work." Anyone could pray in that general way, but only you have the heart to really uncover what you want to ask God to do for your husband that would make him dance and shout for joy and then to pray specifically for those things.

Here's how it works in our marriage in one area. When I travel to speak at a nonprofit organization's fund-raising events, I always ask Darlene to pray for the specific amount that the organization and board hopes will be raised. Darlene intercedes for me, and as a result, I can often sense heaven's power and pleasure.

At times when I'm speaking at a major function and I can sense some spiritual opposition, I'll text Darlene, "Pray, really struggling!" and she will often stop everything and kneel, begging God for protection and freedom for me. Often I feel complete freedom within two minutes and text her back my deep appreciation. Do I ever feel helped!

As I fulfill my role as president of Teach Every Nation, Darlene prays that we'll be able to open a dozen new nations this year, open 1,000 new training centers, and add an additional 50,000 new students. Do you know why she knows those numbers? Because she cares enough about me to ask and then goes to the throne of God and asks God to make those very things happen. Her prayers are so vital to our success.

Do you know the specifics that would mean the world to your husband if they came true this year? This month? This week? Sadly, I've discovered that very few women have any idea about their husband's work life except when he's late. Again.

Secret #2: Appeal to God to help your husband overcome his problems.

Your husband struggles with personal and professional challenges and problems that discourage and weaken him. If your husband isn't facing at least one problem, then wait until tomorrow! Just imagine how your husband will feel when he discovers that you care so much for him that you'll help shoulder the weight with him.

Whether the issue is an arrogant boss, unreasonable "top-down" impossible goals, a lack of money to pay the car insurance this month, a brother who always tears him down in front of others, or exhaustion because his long-awaited vacation just happened to fall on the very day his aging mother fell, breaking her hip, and he had to cancel everything and drive 400 miles to help her all week... You get the idea!

Often you will be aware of these issues because you live together and so you can immediately pick up on and bring his disappointment or discouragement or frustration or anger to God and appeal for God's comfort and intervention.

It's okay for you to not share your prayers with him and just let them be your secret, between you and God, done in your "closet" where you pray and intercede on his behalf.

Three hours ago, my wife came down to my office as I was finishing up a very difficult e-mail to a person who unfortunately has turned out to lack integrity. She knew of the brewing problem, and I asked her to read the e-mail to give me wise counsel. "Was I too direct? Was I off base? Did I deal with the root issue with grace?" Before she left to go back to our home, she offered a prayer with me for God to intervene and redeem a painful problem that I've been unable to solve. Now, as I'm re-editing this chapter, I'm delighted to report that her prayers were answered. Again.

Maybe you sense your husband struggles with pornography. Maybe the new young secretary seems to have some extra affection for your husband. Maybe he gets so discouraged that he has been stopping at the bar on the way home to drown his distress in too many drinks. Maybe he's starting to lose his hair and his previously perfectly toned body now sags and he's feeling like a has-been and overdoses every night on football, baseball, or basketball TV marathons. Maybe he's facing real problems with one of your children and can't seem to find the answer. All these problems are prevalent in our society today, aren't they?

No matter who your husband is, he faces many of these temptations, like every other man. Appeal to God to protect your husband from the temptations he's most vulnerable to and ask God to fill him with extra comfort. Focus not on attacking him but on protecting him. Comfort him so that his inner strength will increase and he will have the courage to say no when tempted.

Can you list three challenging problems that you know your husband is currently struggling with?

You don't have to tell him, "I want to pray for you about this." Just be one with your husband and care enough to find out either in conversation or through your discernment what challenges he is dealing with. How on earth can a wife help her husband with his major problems if she doesn't even know about them?

Secret #3: Appeal to God to transform your husband into the image of Christ.

This is a most powerful type of praying. Instead of nagging, go right over your husband's head and ask God to do the very thing that He wants—to transform your husband more and more to be like Jesus in his character and conduct. Because this is exactly the will of God for your husband—when you pray like this, you know you are right in heaven's bull's-eye.

Read Galatians 5:22-23 and ask God to develop each of the fruit of the Spirit in your husband's personal life: "The fruit of the Spirit is love, joy, peace, longsuffering, kindness, goodness, faithfulness, gentleness, self-control" (NKJV).

Find the one character quality you know your husband wishes was true of him, and make that your primary prayer focus. Do you see how dramatically different this way of thinking and praying really is? Instead of praying for the one quality you wish your husband had, turn your focus to your husband; he's the one you are called to help. And he undoubtedly wants help in an area that probably isn't your number one! Put his wishes first and God will take notice of your unselfish request, and take care of you as well.

Some years ago, Darlene and I selected one character quality of Christ and then focused on that with God, with each other, and in our prayers. One year I desired more patience, another more love, and most recently more kindness. A few months ago, I asked Darlene one evening if she felt I had grown in my kindness. She smiled and said, "Absolutely! Both of us can probably stop praying for that one now!"

One of the most freeing things that can happen in a wife's life occurs when she releases her husband into the hands of Jesus and then asks Him directly to take care of him and change him. She releases the internal push to "make" her husband better and instead appeals to the only One who can transform anyone. Such amazing peace she will have.

Secret #4: Appeal to God to draw your husband into a closer relationship with Christ.

Ultimately, when your husband starts drawing closer to Christ on a regular basis, the Spirit of God will empower him in every area of his life to his benefit and to your delight. Unless your husband is highly unusual, he probably doesn't cater to your "pushing" him to be more spiritual. But when the Spirit of God "pulls" him to Himself, your man may shock you and head in that direction with a willing heart.

Appeal to the Spirit of God to increase His "pulling" and "drawing" of your husband to Himself. Tell Him you trust Him with your husband and claim the promise that Christ will "complete" what He starts (Philippians 1:6 NKJV). Ask God to surprise your husband by unexpectedly pouring His love right into his heart more and more.

Ask God to forgive your husband of his many past and present sins and choose to overwhelm him with His mercy and compassion. Ask the Godhead to communicate to your husband through any method He would like—to make Himself known directly to your husband.

If you find yourself complaining and pushing your husband toward God, stop immediately and bite your tongue. You are pushing your husband away. Don't appeal to him to pursue God unless he brings his desires up to you. Appeal to the heavenly Father directly on his behalf.

Secret #5: Appeal to God to lead your husband to be the loving head of your marriage and family.

If my guess is correct, this would be number one on your list rather than number five. Why, then, did I place it last? It's not that I don't agree to its high importance, because I do, but for another reason. I've discovered that if there are positive movements on Secrets 1-4, your husband cannot help but become a more loving head of your marriage and family.

But without positive improvement in those previous areas, your husband may not feel worthy to lead or may not want to shoulder more responsibility than he already is facing at work or may be overwhelmed by the problems and sins he is already dealing with. He may arrive home wanting to hide and forget his troubles rather than to rise up with inner strength to help you and the children and grandchildren.

Once again, however, I'm not excusing your husband's selfishness or abdication of his God-given responsibilities and dumping them on you. Instead, I'm encouraging you to reconsider how you seek to achieve what you long for in your man by the order of things you pray for.

Husbands seem to stiffen whenever their wives confront them on spiritual matters, especially on being the "spiritual head of the home." If your husband grew up without his father and was raised only by his mother, he will find being the "head" way out of his comfort zone. If your husband grew up with an aloof or abusive and disconnected father, then he likely will have inbred traits and expectations that will need tender care to reshape, often with two steps forward and one-and-a-half steps backward.

Beg God to grant your husband courage. Ask God to instill experiences that breed confidence instead of defeat. Accept your husband exactly where he is, and then start helping him. See what God can do!

Look back to Secrets 1 and 2 and start appealing to God to intervene and get some exciting answers to prayer. Then spread out and move down the other secrets because you will know that your prayers really do make a major difference in the life of your husband.

Chapter Five

Using Your Mantle Effectively

I'm so glad that you have stayed with me to this point! I'm sure you would readily admit that these chapters do not reflect the thoughts and attitudes of most married women in the world today—but they come directly from the Word of God, don't they? That's why wives who live according to the timeless teachings of God about their roles always stand out above the rest. They enjoy the blessings from God!

Tragically, the clearly defined biblical roles of "head" and "helper" have slowly disappeared from society and most churches. Take a moment and reflect. When was the last time, on any television program, that you saw a wife working to support and help her husband, let alone praying for her husband? Probably never.

Will you then break the mold and trust God enough to appeal to Him in prayer so you can multiply your "helpfulness" to a huge degree? When you do, your husband will notice over time that he has changed in numerous ways and has become more successful, and you will be the secret recipient of God's unique pleasure and blessings as you fulfilled His design and dreams for you.

I can promise you as the husband of a remarkable wife, I am forever grateful for a godly woman who helped me become someone I never could have become without her loyal and unconditional love and help.

Here are a few helpful tips that can make these Mantle prayers work easily and effectively for you:

- Don't allow yourself to be overwhelmed by all these new thoughts. Start with a couple ideas and watch what happens. Pick out two to three things from Secrets 1-2 and enjoy some victories!

- Buy a little notebook that you keep confidential from everyone and start tracking God's answers to your specific appeals. The following is a method you might try, which is one I have used for many years. Here's an example:

  1. Please, God, help my husband to make the big sale this week. 7/1/17 YES! 7/4/17 3 days

  Number the first prayer and continue numbering every time you add another request.

  Put the date next to it when you started praying it: 7/1/17.

  When God answers with a "yes" or "no," then write it on the right side of your request: YES!

  Then put the date God answered your prayer: 7/4/17.

  Estimate how many days you prayed until God answered: 3 days.

  Put a star next to the number when you pray extra hard for it that day: *.

  Then circle the number every time God answers

with a "yes." It will shock you how many "yesses" you receive!

- Every day when you pray, pray through your prayers quickly unless your heart tugs that you need to ask more fervently on one of them. Then simply tell God why that particular prayer request is so important to you. It will make a difference! Place a star next to that number whenever you pray more fervently. Some of my most important prayers have many stars.

- When you are finished praying through your list, ask yourself one simple question: "What else do I sense my husband is wishing for?" Think for a few moments and you'll be wonderfully surprised how the Lord will help you know what He wants you to pray for your husband. Then just number the next one in your list, pray for it, and go on with your business for the day.

- How long should your prayers take? Just a couple of minutes. Really? Yes. Just talk to God and make your requests known. Ask Him and don't be shy or timid. You are doing exactly what He wants! He loves hearing from you.

- Do this for 30 days in row. If you ask the question "What else does my husband wish for?" after you quickly pray through your list, you will be shocked that after 30 days you will have dozens of specific requests! And better than that, you will likely have many "Yes!" answers.

- Never write a general request in your Husband Prayer Notebook. Why not? Because how will you know if God answered it or not?

- Learn to ask specific questions of your husband to discover his wishes, like, "If you could get one to two key results this week, what would you want?" Don't tell him you are going to pray about them unless he is open to that.

- On every Sunday afternoon for four weeks, read through these short introductory chapters. You will find much help and encouragement every time you do.

- Begin meditating on the secrets I wrote about in chapter 4 and try to write at least a couple requests in your Husband Prayer Notebook from each of the five categories.

- At the end of the 30 days, look down your long list and celebrate and thank God for all His "Yes!" and all His equally good "No!" answers. You will be amazed at how many times God came through for you. And you will never again wonder if prayer really works. You'll have so much proof in your notebook you'll never want to stop!

Finally, I would like to share a brief closing word about some powerful truths that can radically improve your prayer life. Too many people either misunderstand or have emotional uncertainty regarding two of the primary purposes for praying for your husband: to get answers and to receive something you really want for your husband. If you don't want a prayer answered, then certainly don't pray it or write it in your notebook!

Far too many of us think that praying for what we desire must be selfish, or perhaps inappropriate. Because we know we should pray but somehow feel guilty about praying for what we wish would happen, we never find full release in praying. But read what Jesus stated about praying for what you desire: "If you abide in Me, and My words abide in you, *you will ask what you desire*, and it shall be done for you" (John 15:7 NKJV, emphasis added).

In this verse, Jesus revealed a very strategic secret: When you abide in Christ, and His Word is in you, you can ask for whatever you desire. Because when you abide in Him, His desires will be your desires.

In this way, Jesus uncovers one of the secrets of prayer:

> **Your desires should turn into your prayers. Ask for what you desire.**

In fact, one of the most surprising insights I have ever had about prayer is that the more that I abide in Christ and the more His words abide in me, the more I am fully and completely released to pray for everything I desire. Jesus connected abiding with Christ and obedience to His commands as the underlying cause of asking for what you desire.

> **If you abide, you will ask what you desire!**

You aren't instructed to pray for things merely because you know you are supposed to—like an obligation. Instead, Jesus expressly states you are to ask for whatever you want. If you want something, then ask and don't stop asking until you get an answer, whether that's yes or no.

When Jesus stated, "Ask what you desire," He put the word *ask* in the present active tense, which means He was saying to pray when you want something and then keep on praying for it until you receive God's answer. That's why I suggested that after you pray through your list for your husband, pause for a second and ask, "What else does my husband wish for?" When you add the next request to your prayers, you are obeying Christ's clear instructions. Abandon yourself to pray for anything that you desire for your husband and yourself!

Jesus promised that when you pray for whatever you desire and God answers that prayer, your heart will explode with fullness of joy: "Until now you have asked nothing in My name. *Ask*, and you will receive, *that your joy may be full*" (John 16:24 NKJV, emphasis added).

Joy always follows when any of us receive what we deeply desire in relation to what God might want to do for us. Too few believers experience joy in their walk with God because they aren't continually asking God for the things they desire. The more you get in contact with your many desires provided they are scriptural, the more you should put them on your prayer list and ask the Lord to grant them to you and your husband, and then the more opportunities God will have to answer your requests. The more answers you get to your prayers, the more joy will flow through your life—and also to your husband as he receives the blessing of getting something he wished!

By the way, if you constantly worry about whether your prayer is valid, never forget one foundational truth: If God doesn't want to answer your prayer, He won't! You cannot sin by making your desires known to Him, but you can sin by not making your desires know to Him! So stop asking yourself, "Should I pray for that?" and just ask, realizing God is never upset by your desires, as He already knows them!

In closing the chapters on the Wife's Mantle, do you know what would fill me with joy? If someday at a conference or at Starbucks you saw me and came over and shared your joy of how you excelled as your husband's amazing helper and even told me, "Thus far I've gotten 73 'Yes!' answers to my prayers and I can hardly recognize my husband! My heart is overflowing with joy!"

Part 2

Taking On the
Mantle of Prayer

Taking On the Mantle of Prayer

Are you ready to start using your Mantle more fully? We want to come alongside you to help you do just that and have included 50 different topics in this section for you to pray over. You can choose the one or ones you feel most relate to your husband's needs right now or you can move through them progressively, picking a new topic every day. Simply read the next Prayer for your husband and pray the prayer with women all over the world. This isn't meant to be time-consuming or overwhelming; just read and then pray. We've also included some suggestions to guide you as you pray specifically for your husband.

We have divided each day into three sections after the pattern for prayer found in 2 Chronicles 20:6-12.

Section One: Praising God (2 Chronicles 20:6-9)

"Lord, the God of our ancestors, are you not the God who is in heaven? You rule over all the kingdoms of the nations. Power and might are in your hand, and no one can withstand you. Our God, did you not drive out the inhabitants of this land before your people Israel and give it forever to the descendants of Abraham your friend? They have lived in it and have built in it a sanctuary for your Name, saying, 'If calamity comes upon us, whether the sword of judgment, or plague or famine, we will stand in your presence before this temple that bears your Name and will cry out to you in our distress, and you will hear us and save us.'"

Section Two: Presenting the Situation (2 Chronicles 20:10-11)

"But now here are men from Ammon, Moab and Mount Seir, whose territory you would not allow Israel to invade when they came from Egypt; so they turned away from them and did not destroy them. See how they are repaying us by coming to drive us out of the possession you gave us as an inheritance."

Section Three: Praying for Blessing and Intervention (2 Chronicles 20:12)

"Our God, will you not judge them? For we have no power to face this vast army that is attacking us. We do not know what to do, but our eyes are upon you."

———

This is not some magical pattern meant to be used so that your prayers will come true. But it is an established pattern in Scripture for how to approach the throne of God and talk to Him about your needs. Remember, the main thing is your abiding relationship with Jesus Christ. But this pattern serves as a structure we've used in guiding wives around the world to help them zero in on more specific, regular, and affirming prayers for their husbands. We pray that as your prayer journey continues to develop more fully, God Himself will bless you with a supernatural covering and the motivation to pray regularly, fervently, and with great expectation!

1

Character: Love

*"The fruit of the Spirit is love...Against such
things there is no law"* (Galatians 5:22-23).

Praising God

Heavenly Father, You are love. First John 4:8 tells us, 'Whoever does not love does not know God, because God is love.' Your essence and totality are made up of love. You embody the traits of love that we should live out—traits such as patience, kindness, gentleness, humility, and self-control (1 Corinthians 13). I praise You because of Your commitment to love me and to love my spouse in spite of the many ways we may have failed You. I praise You because Your love tempers Your anger toward us and we can appeal to Your faithful love when we need it the most. Your love enables us to experience Your forgiveness and blessing, along with Your mercy and favor. Thank You for Your love and for giving us the opportunity to model Your love to each other."

Presenting the Situation

Use this portion of your prayer to the Lord to share with Him about your specific situation related to love. You may want to ask God to open your eyes to see where your spouse may need to grow with regard to loving Him and loving you more fully. You can also ask God to give you insight into the ways your husband is loving you but you may not be aware of. We all understand love through our own grids of perception. Ask God to help you recognize those times when your husband is showing you love that you may not be recognizing on your own, and ask Him to develop in you an appreciation for the ways your husband shows you love.

Praying for Blessing and Intervention

Gracious Lord, I ask that You bless my husband with a spirit of love. Bless his actions, thoughts, and words with Your love so that he reflects Your love to himself, to me, and to others. Help him to love You with all his heart, soul, and mind. Help him to love me more deeply, more passionately, and even more spontaneously. Revive and restore the "first love" he once felt for me when we began to date or started our relationship together. Expand his understanding of what true love looks like. Bless my husband with the ability to love himself purely as well. In Christ's name, amen.

2

Character: Joy

"The fruit of the Spirit is…joy…Against such things there is no law" (Galatians 5:22-23).

Praising God

Heavenly Father, joy is found in You. Psalm 16:11 tells me, 'You make known to me the path of life; you will fill me with joy in your presence, with eternal pleasures at your right hand.' I praise You for being the source of joy not only for myself but for my husband. I know that You will make known to him the path of life and You will fill him with joy as he abides in Your presence. Thank You that the attainment of true joy is found in You and that joy is available to him at any time. First Chronicles 16:27 assures me that 'splendor and majesty are before him [God]; strength and joy are in his dwelling place.' My husband can gain both strength and joy simply by remaining in Your presence. You have blessed us with access to You, and I honor Your name in praise."

Presenting the Situation

Use this portion to bring specific concerns, circumstances, or challenges your husband may be facing with this character quality of joy. Ask the Lord to address these particular areas with His grace and to draw your husband closer into His presence, which is the source of all joy. Share with God some ways you have witnessed your husband display this quality of joy and thank Him for them. Then finish this time by asking for wisdom and insight on how you can be an encouragement to your husband in these areas you've brought up.

Praying for Blessing and Intervention

> Gracious Lord, I pray for my husband according to Romans 15:13, "May the God of hope fill [him] with all joy and peace as [he trusts in You], so that [he] may overflow with hope by the power of the Holy Spirit." Flood my husband's spirit with the fullness and power of Your joy. Give him experiences that reignite his playful side. Allow me the chance to be a part of You bringing him joy. I want to see him smile, laugh, and delight in the abundance of blessings You have given us each day. May our home and our marriage be known for the joy we share together. And may that joy overflow into the lives of those around us, for Your glory and their good. In Christ's name, amen.

Character: Peace

*"The fruit of the Spirit is…peace…Against such
things there is no law"* (Galatians 5:22-23).

Praising God

Heavenly Father, Your peace protects, provides for, and promotes greater harmony and satisfaction in our marriage. I praise You for peace that guards us according to Philippians 4:7: 'And the peace of God, which transcends all understanding, will guard your hearts and your minds in Christ Jesus.' Accessing Your peace is as simple as focusing on You. 'You will keep in perfect peace those whose minds are steadfast, because they trust in you' (Isaiah 26:3). Thank You for the gift of peace through Jesus Christ and what it will accomplish in my husband's life, in his thoughts, and in his heart. 'Peace I leave with you; my peace I give you. I do not give to you as the world gives. Do not let your hearts be troubled and do not be afraid' (John 14:27)."

Presenting the Situation

Use this portion to direct your thoughts to specific areas in your husband's life where he may be struggling to experience peace. Also talk with the Lord about how his lack of peace impacts you, your marriage, and your home. Ask God to intervene specifically in this area, whether that's in a job situation, your relationship, or even his inner conflict. Areas that can often produce a loss of peace in husbands can include feelings of a lack of purpose, a loss of direction, an inability to fulfill their role well, or even insignificance.

Praying for Blessing and Intervention

Gracious Lord, fill my husband with Your peace. Help him to recognize Your presence in his life more fully and guide him in focusing his mind on You rather than on the worries of this world. Give him an unshakable confidence in You as our source of peace and as our provider so that he can rest in You. Make me a model of peace to him by giving me the grace of a gentle spirit. Help us both to look to You first before responding or reacting to each other out of our emotions, especially emotions of worry, fear, anxiety, or disappointment. You promise us perfect peace when our minds are focused on You. I ask that You cultivate in my husband a desire to pray with me and lead me spiritually so that we develop the habit and routine of always focusing on You. In Christ's name, amen.

Character: Forbearance

"The fruit of the Spirit is…forbearance…Against such things there is no law" (Galatians 5:22-23).

Praising God

Heavenly Father, it is Your forbearance that gives us life and frees us from the wrath that is due us because of our sins. There exists no greater model of forbearance than Your willingness to offer Your Son, Jesus Christ, and His death on the cross as a sacrifice while we were yet sinners and blinded to Your greatness, holiness, and love. Without Your forbearance, none of us could last even a moment. The simple response You desire from us for this great gift is our praise. As it says in Isaiah 48:9, 'For my own name's sake I delay my wrath; for the sake of my praise I hold it back from you, so as not to destroy you completely.' I give You praise and gratitude for Your forbearance, Lord, not only in my life but also in my husband's life and in our marriage."

Presenting the Situation

Use this portion to pray about those areas of your relationship where judgment, blame, accusation, and resentment have made themselves known. These negative emotional responses can damage any relationship. Ask God for His forgiveness on behalf of both of you and ask for His healing where a lack of forbearance may have surfaced from a hurt or wound. Be sure to bring up specific situations where healing may need to take place or where one of you is quick to criticize and blame the other in your relationship. Ask for wisdom and insight on how to curtail those situations and get ahead of them so that they no longer present themselves as an opportunity for your actions to bring destruction into your marriage.

Praying for Blessing and Intervention

> Gracious Lord, no marriage relationship is perfect. There are times when I offend my spouse and he offends me, simply because we are human. Give us both the grace to keep the virtue of forbearance first and foremost in our thoughts about each other and our words with each other. Help my husband to have forbearance with other members of our family as well. Nurture his relationship with You because it is out of his closeness with the Holy Spirit that this fruit will manifest in him. Show me opportunities to express my admiration and gratitude to him for the times his forbearance blesses our home. In Christ's name, amen.

Character: Kindness

"The fruit of the Spirit is…kindness…Against such things there is no law" (Galatians 5:22-23).

Praising God

Heavenly Father, You have told us what is good and what You require of us during our days on earth. We are to do justice, love kindness, and walk humbly with You (Micah 6:8). Loving-kindness means treating all people with respect and protecting other people's emotions. It also means encouraging others in a way that helps them to develop into a fuller image of Christ. You model the kindness described in Romans 2:4: 'Or do you show contempt for the riches of his kindness, forbearance and patience, not realizing that God's kindness is intended to lead you to repentance?' I praise You for Your kindness, and thank You for how in my own life and in my husband's life it draws us closer to You and leads us to repent of the areas where we have been unkind."

Presenting the Situation

Use this portion to bring before the Lord in prayer any areas of your relationship where you feel that kindness may be missing. It could show up in a lack of kindness to others, not only with each other. Kindness is the hallmark of spiritual maturity because it is rooted in respect and humility. Ask God to reveal to you and your spouse ways in which you can both grow and develop in the area of kindness.

Praying for Blessing and Intervention

Gracious Lord, I ask that You will guide and instruct my husband in the ways of kindness. Let the meditations of his heart and the words of his mouth always be pleasing to You. I pray that his actions will model a heart of humility that is reflected in kindness. Develop a mutual spirit of kindness between us, guarding us from speaking or doing anything cruel, mean, or even dismissive to each other. May my husband be kind to his co-workers, our family members, and those he comes across through the activities of everyday life. Help me to be an encouragement to him in this area and make me a model of what kindness looks like, sounds like, and feels like in our home. Reveal to my husband those times when he is acting or speaking unkindly to me, even though he may not be aware of it. Let Your Spirit convict him and lead him into a deeper level of expression of kindness in our relationship. In Christ's name, amen.

6

Character: Goodness

*"The fruit of the Spirit is...goodness...Against such
things there is no law"* (Galatians 5:22-23).

Praising God

Heavenly Father, You are good, a stronghold in the day of
trouble. You know those who take refuge in Your goodness (Nahum 1:7). Because of this You instruct us to turn from
what is wrong and negative and to do good instead (Psalm
34:14). Goodness spreads peace to those around us. I praise You
for instructing us in the ways of goodness through Your Word.
My husband will enjoy his life and our family much more fully
when he trusts in You and does good, because You have promised this result in Scripture (Psalm 37:3). Thank You for Your
promises, for giving us a road map to living life fully and with
abounding goodness."

Presenting the Situation

Use this portion to consider any areas of your marriage
where goodness has prevailed. Take time to thank God for these
areas. Also consider ways that your husband does good to those
around him, whether that is to you, your family members, your
church community, or his co-workers. Look for ways to build

him up by telling him of your respect and admiration for the things he does that are good. Ask God to give you a special insight into how you can encourage your husband by recognizing the spirit of goodness in him.

Praying for Blessing and Intervention

> Gracious Lord, thank You for all the ways that my husband is good. Thank You for allowing me to experience his goodness on many levels. I pray that You will increase his goodness that he shows to others—whether it be to me in our marriage, to our family members, or with other people with whom he interacts. Your Word says, "So then, while we have opportunity, let us do good to all people, and especially to those who are of the household of the faith" (Galatians 6:10 NASB). Give my husband wisdom on how he can best use his time, talents, and resources to be an influence of good in our marriage, church body, or small group. Also show him how he can do good to others who need it, maybe through mission opportunities or in meeting community needs. Help me support him as You lead him in this area. In Christ's name, amen.

7

Character: Faithfulness

*"The fruit of the Spirit is…faithfulness…Against
such things there is no law"* (Galatians 5:22-23).

Praising God

Heavenly Father, Your attribute of faithfulness shows up in multiple ways. It nourishes fellowship, provides the flow of blessing, and withholds Your judgment. I praise You for Your faithfulness to me throughout my life, and Your faithfulness to my husband as well. First Corinthians 1:9 says, 'God is faithful, who has called you into fellowship with his Son, Jesus Christ our Lord.' And Deuteronomy 7:9 says of Your faithfulness, 'Know therefore that the LORD your God is God; he is the faithful God, keeping his covenant of love to a thousand generations of those who love him and keep his commandments.' Because of Your great love, we are not consumed. Your compassions never fail. Each day and every morning we wake up to experience more of Your great faithfulness (Lamentations 3:22-23). Thank You, Lord, that we never have to feel frightened and that we can trust Your faithfulness."

Presenting the Situation

Use this portion as an opportunity to thank God for the

areas in your husband's life where he has demonstrated faithfulness in his character. This can include faithfulness to his roles of leader, provider, and protector. It could also include his faithfulness to be the spiritual head of the home. If there are areas where your husband still needs to develop, then use this time as an opportunity to ask God to pinpoint those areas in his life and mature your husband into the man He is calling him to be. If your husband has been unfaithful to you in any way, use this time to ask the Lord to bring him to repentance and to help you heal from the wounds that his unfaithfulness has created in you. Ask God to restore trust between the both of you and to provide you with tangible ways of being reassured where you feel insecure due to unfaithfulness.

Praying for Blessing and Intervention

> Gracious Lord, thank You for the many ways that my husband has been faithful to me and to our family over the years. I pray that You will help me express my gratitude to him in such a way that causes him to truly feel esteemed and respected by me. In the areas where he still needs to grow, Lord, I ask that You arrange situations and circumstances in his life that will cultivate this virtue more deeply in him. Give me wisdom on how to model faithfulness in a way that will be appealing to him. And where either of us has broken trust in each other, I ask for Your supernatural healing hand to restore that trust. Lord, heal the wounds unfaithfulness has caused so that we do not hurt each other even more deeply by responding out of pain rather than out of love and faithfulness. In Christ's name, amen.

8

Character: Gentleness

"The fruit of the Spirit is…gentleness…Against such things there is no law" (Galatians 5:22-23).

Praising God

Heavenly Father, You ask us to let our gentleness be evident to all because You are near (Philippians 4:5). That tells me You enjoy environments where gentleness is the dominant atmosphere because it reflects Your nature. I praise and honor You for having such a gentle Spirit in the face of so much rebellion, disobedience, and distraction by those You have created. You ask us to do the same. Colossians 3:12 says, 'Therefore, as God's chosen people, holy and dearly loved, clothe yourselves with compassion, kindness, humility, gentleness and patience.' I pray that I will clothe myself in such a way that I reflect You to my husband, and always help me to respond to him with a gentle answer because that turns away frustration, but a harsh response stirs up anger (Proverbs 15:1)."

Presenting the Situation

Use this portion to take some time and examine your own heart and actions as a wife. Does gentleness rule all that you say and do? Can you tell a difference in the times when you respond to your husband with a gentle spirit versus those times when you allow your negative emotions to cause a much harsher response? Identify these areas and ask God to grace you with His favor by helping you to embody what it truly means to be a gentle, trusting, humble spirit. After you've prayed about yourself, spend some time praying and asking the Lord to cultivate these virtues in your husband as well.

Praying for Blessing and Intervention

Gracious Lord, so much needless conflict could be avoided in our marriage if we made a spirit of gentleness the rule of thumb for all of our interactions. Help my husband to be gentle in all he says and does. Help me to be the same. In those times when I have been hurt because he has not spoken to me in a gentle tone or with gentle words, I ask that You help me to forgive and let that go. Enable us to spend time hugging or doing what we each need to do in order to calm down when we become upset, so that we can address each other with words and gestures that embody gentleness. In Christ's name, amen.

9

Character: Self-Control

"The fruit of the Spirit is…self-control…Against such things there is no law" (Galatians 5:22-23).

Praising God

Heavenly Father, I praise You for the wisdom You have in providing Your Spirit to develop the fruit of self-control in us. Without self-control, we will charge ahead in ways that can be destructive to ourselves and those around us. Self-control enables us to watch what we say and do so that we are respectful and kind and gracious in our words. It keeps us from doing things that would hurt each other in our marriage. It gives us the strength to form healthy boundaries in different areas of our lives. Thank You for giving us the gift of this spiritual fruit, Lord, and I ask that my husband will cherish it as much as You do. May it be the hallmark of our relationship together."

Presenting the Situation

Use this portion to talk to the Lord about any areas of your marriage or your husband's life where an additional amount of self-control could bring about a greater benefit in your home. It may revolve around eating, gaming, conversing, binge-watching of the television, how he speaks to you, how he speaks to others, how he interacts with family members, spending, working, relationships with the opposite sex, etc. Let the Lord know the target areas you are asking Him to address in your husband's life and pray for wisdom on how you can be supportive of the work He is doing in your husband's heart.

Praying for Blessing and Intervention

> Gracious Lord, I ask that You pour out an abundance of the fruit of self-control into my husband's spirit—covering his words, actions, thoughts, desires, and reactions with this grace. Set a guard around his heart and emotions so that he does not simply respond to what life throws at him but that he uses wisdom to respond appropriately in ways that bring about edification for himself and those all around him, including me. Keep me from being a stumbling block to him in this area and keep me from complaining about any lack of self-control he exhibits in any way. Rather, let me look to You to guide him and restrain him in all ways that he needs to be guided and self-controlled as I put my trust in You. Thank You, God. In Christ's name, amen.

10

Courage: Waging Spiritual Warfare

"Be strong in the Lord and in his mighty power. Put on the full armor of God, so that you can take your stand against the devil's schemes. For our struggle is not against flesh and blood, but against the rulers, against the authorities, against the powers of this dark world and against the spiritual forces of evil in the heavenly realms" (Ephesians 6:10-12).

Praising God

Heavenly Father, my husband's strength and his courage are to come directly from You. You teach us that we are to be 'strong in the Lord and in his mighty power.' Courage and confidence are rooted and grounded in a love relationship with Jesus Christ. So I praise You that through the sacrifice and resurrection of Christ, my husband has direct access to You in order to tap into all that You are and all that You are willing to share with him. Thank You for Your abundant power and the reality that You are the one who is ultimately waging warfare in the spiritual realms on our behalf. I praise You that my husband is not fighting for victory but rather he is fighting from a position of victory—the victory You have already achieved on our behalf."

Presenting the Situation

Use this portion to reflect on areas where your husband has shown courage in your home, in your marriage, at work, or in any issues that he has faced. Thank God specifically for these times and ask God to strengthen your husband in any areas where you feel he may still need to grow in obtaining greater courage. Be sure to focus on specific areas where you believe your husband may be under spiritual attack and intervene on his behalf to ask the Lord to give him the tools, wisdom, and strength he needs to face it and overcome it well.

Praying for Blessing and Intervention

Gracious Lord, I pray that You will give my husband the wisdom and courage to put on the full armor of spiritual weapons rather than try to fight the issues and circumstances he faces in his own strength. Help him to understand that it takes great courage to wage war spiritually with the unseen forces. Remind him that faith is an act of courage in and of itself. My husband's struggles are not what he nor I can see; instead, they are struggles against the rulers, authorities, powers of this dark world, and the spiritual forces of evil. To overcome these, he must battle with Your might, not his. Make me his encourager and help me to be a gentle reminder to him on where to focus in times of conflict so that we can both walk in the courageous victory that is ours in Christ Jesus, our Lord. In Christ's name, amen.

11

Courage: Overcoming Challenges

"Put on the full armor of God, so that when the day of evil comes, you may be able to stand your ground, and after you have done everything, to stand" (Ephesians 6:13).

Praising God

Heavenly Father, my husband is able to stand his ground when he is fully equipped with Your spiritual armor. Your Word gives us the confidence to know that our victory lies securely in You. You have overcome Satan and the enemy's attacks on Your children. You have assisted and provided for countless numbers of people to overcome attacks on them as well. I know that You will enable and strengthen my husband to overcome all that the enemy tries to throw his way in an effort to defeat him and to derail our marriage and family. I praise You that my confidence rests in You."

Presenting the Situation

Use this portion to ask God to open your eyes and heart to see any challenges your husband may be facing individually or challenges you may be facing in your marriage through a spiritual lens. Ask the Lord to give you restraint from blaming your husband for struggles or troubles in your marriage and to give you the ability to discern the root behind those troubles. As God gives you specific situations to think about, pray that He will cover and equip your husband fully with His armor and train him on how to use each piece effectively.

Praying for Blessing and Intervention

Gracious Lord, I pray that You will give my husband a desire to put on the armor You have provided and supplied for him. Help him to recognize the courage it takes to wage spiritual warfare. Enlighten his mind and his heart to spiritual matters. Bring teachings and conversations along his path that can further mentor and develop him in this area. Surround him with relationships that reinforce Your mind-set of how we are to both face and overcome challenges in life. Cause me to speak and act in such a way that encourages his development in this area and helps him achieve success in spiritual warfare. In Christ's name, amen.

12

Conflict: The Power of Truth, Righteousness, and Peace

"Stand firm then, with the belt of truth buckled around your waist, with the breastplate of righteousness in place, and with your feet fitted with the readiness that comes from the gospel of peace" (Ephesians 6:14-15).

Praising God

Heavenly Father, thank You for Your attributes of truth, righteousness, and peace. These underlying qualities—when used correctly—can dispel conflict almost instantly. I praise You that You embody such traits and make them available to us in our everyday lives. It is because of Your righteousness that my husband is able to approach Your throne of grace boldly, on behalf of himself, our marriage, our home, and in all his other activities and interactions. You tell us that Your peace will both rule and guard our hearts in Christ Jesus, giving us the opportunity to find a way out of conflict without allowing conflict to bring destruction into our spirits and into our relationship with each other. Help us to seek that peace and depend on You in the full armor that You provide so that we may truly live in peace."

Presenting the Situation

Use this portion of your time with God to thank Him for

the different ways your husband handles conflict in a healthy manner. Focus on the times when he sought to discern the truth before jumping to conclusions during times of conflict and express your gratitude for how this positively impacted your marriage and home. Ask God to address any specific needs or areas of needed growth in your husband's life with regard to his desire to discover truth, express righteousness (right living), and walk in a manner of internal and external peace.

Praying for Blessing and Intervention

Gracious Lord, I ask that You will enable us as a couple to refrain from drawing conclusions, making assumptions, or reacting emotionally when we have not yet sought to clarify the cause of our conflict. Remind us to always seek to understand both the truth of the actions and the intentions behind the actions. Help my husband to make right choices throughout his work life, home life, and social life so that the enemy does not have a stronghold from which to attack our family. Let righteousness guard my husband from immoral advances of other women, pornography, or immoral thoughts and desires he may experience for other women. Surround him with Your breastplate of righteousness to protect his honor and heart. And when conflict does arise, let peace both dominate and preserve the sanctity of our relationship and intimacy of our communication and love of the truth. In Christ's name, amen.

13

Conflict: Tools of Faith and Trust

"In addition to all this, take up the shield of faith, with which you can extinguish all the flaming arrows of the evil one. Take the helmet of salvation..." (Ephesians 6:16-17).

Praising God

Heavenly Father, it is impossible to please You without faith. You tell us that anyone who comes to You must believe that You exist and that You reward those who earnestly seek You (Hebrews 11:6). Yet faith is something so very intangible in nature. It is often difficult to conceive. It is the confidence in what we hope for and the assurance of what we do not see (Hebrews 11:1). I praise You for providing an opportunity for us to please You, and for my husband to have access to all he needs to extinguish all that the enemy throws at him, and at us. I pray that his faith will not rest in human wisdom but rather in Your power, Lord (1 Corinthians 2:5), so that we can testify to the greatness of Your strength in our home and in our lives."

Presenting the Situation

Use this portion to thank God for the times He came through for you or for your husband in response to the faith you demonstrated in Him. Consider the many ways God provided for you when you saw no way to make it on your own. Let God know the areas where you feel vulnerable to the enemy's attacks in your home and where you perceive that your husband may be vulnerable as well. Ask Him to fortify your spouse with a high level of supernatural faith, enabling him to overcome all of the challenges and "darts of the enemy" that come his way.

Praying for Blessing and Intervention

> Gracious Lord, the security of Your salvation means I never need to fear my eternal destiny due to my faith in Christ and His sacrifice. Let that security overflow into the faith that I have in You and how You work in and through my husband for the betterment of our home and our lives. Satan is busy creating triggers of conflict or suspicions, Lord. I ask that the shield of faith become second nature to my husband and to us as a couple so that we gain mastery in seeing past the physical circumstances and into the spiritual root of any conflict we face. Thank You for giving us faith as a vital piece of our armor in our spiritual life so that we can live the abundant life promised to us in Your Son. In Christ's name, amen.

14

Conflict: Using the Word of God

*"...and the sword of the Spirit, which is the
word of God"* (Ephesians 6:17).

Praising God

Heavenly Father, You tell us, 'In the beginning was the Word,
and the Word was with God, and the Word was God. He
was with God in the beginning' (John 1:1-2). It was through
Your Word that all things were made (John 1:3). It was through
Your words that the earth was created, the light shown out of
darkness, the ground was formed, and humanity came into
existence (Genesis 1:1-26). Your Word carries more power than
we can imagine. I praise You, heavenly Father, for the power of
Your Word and the ability You have given us in having access
to it through reading, meditating, and quoting Your Holy
Scripture."

Presenting the Situation

Use this portion to examine how much you and your husband use the Word of God as the sword of the Spirit. Consider
at what level you think of it as a tool to wage warfare against the
enemy or whether it has just become something to read or go
to during times of devotion. Ask God to give your husband a

greater hunger for studying and memorizing God's Word and pray for wisdom on how to use it as a sword of the Spirit in your marriage and home. Meditate on those passages in the Bible where you find strength and victory. Consider writing those key verses on a 3 x 5-inch card and carry them with you so you can read the verses out loud when you are tempted, just like Jesus did when He was tempted.

Praying for Blessing and Intervention

> Gracious Lord, guide my husband through the study of Your Word in such a way that he becomes an expert at understanding and using Your Word for our benefit in our home and for his own personal growth. God, please help him to devote and dedicate time to spend with You in Your Word in the morning hours before the busyness of the day comes upon him. Please also help him to return to Your Word throughout the day and provide ways for me to be an encouragement to him since he is our spiritual leader in the home. I want to encourage him to stay well versed in what You say in Scripture. Give him a fresh experience of You, Lord, and the power of Your living Word. Help him to see You as the relational, relevant God that You are and let Your Word become a weapon that he wields wisely every day. In Christ's name, amen.

15

Conflict: Power of Prayer

*"Pray in the Spirit on all occasions with all kinds of prayers
and requests. With this in mind, be alert and always keep
on praying for all the Lord's people"* (Ephesians 6:18).

Praising God

Heavenly Father, prayer moves mountains and brings life into
situations. It is within our war room of prayer that we find
our greatest tools for change, impact, and conflict resolution. I
give You praise for Your willingness to allow us to approach You
in prayer and Your eagerness to respond to our requests. You say
that all my husband needs to do is to ask, seek, and knock and
You will open the door for him. I know this is true and pray that
he will also know this to be true, and I pray that he will use this
tool to curtail any conflict we have in our marriage and also any
conflict he may face on the job or with friends and other family
members. Thank You for the gift of prayer."

Presenting the Situation

Use this portion to take a look at your prayer life, your husband's prayer life, and your prayer life as a couple. Reread the
first five chapters about the Wife's Mantle again for encouragement and strength. Try to determine how committed you both

are to prayer and how much you incorporate it into your daily routine. Then ask God to increase the areas and times when you are dependent on the tool of prayer. Knowing that prayer is also the abiding mind-set to carry with you always, ask the Lord to bring His viewpoint to bear on the different decisions and responses that your husband needs to make throughout the day. If there is anything specific that he is struggling with or facing right now, ask God to increase both your husband's and your prayers concerning those situations.

Praying for Blessing and Intervention

> Gracious Lord, Your Word says first and foremost that if my husband is not treating me with honor and grace, both of our prayers will be hindered. I desire for our prayers to be heard and answered, Lord, so please give him a heart to treat me according to how You want him to do so (1 Peter 3:7). Help me to cultivate an atmosphere in our home where he trusts me and desires to treat me with kindness and grace. I also ask that You give quick answers to my husband's prayers so that he will see the effectiveness of using this spiritual tool in his life and in our home. Let these answers build upon each other so that his prayer muscles will be strengthened and he will look to prayer as a regular part of living life successfully. Thank You for hearing my prayers for him and for responding. In Christ's name, amen.

16

Character: Love God and Trust Him to Supply Your Needs

"Seek first his kingdom and his righteousness, and all these things will be given to you as well" (Matthew 6:33).

Praising God

Heavenly Father, You are the source of everything we need. You promise that You will supply all of our needs according to Your riches in glory. But You ask that my husband and I put You first as a part of the process of obtaining all that we need. You ask that we seek You first. It is only when You are first in my husband's life that Your provision flows freely through and to him in the marketplace. Thank You for showing us the key that You are the ultimate source of fulfilling our needs, not his work or our finances. Thank You for taking such amazing care of Your creation with the birds and lilies in the fields, and You even know the number of hairs on our heads! I praise You that not only do You make Your unlimited abundance available to us as our Lord, but that You also encourage us to never doubt Your provision and loyal care for us, no matter what the present circumstances may appear to be. I praise You that You do all things well and always have our best interests at heart."

Presenting the Situation

Use this portion to mention to God the times you've seen your husband put Him first. Ask God to show your husband much favor when he makes the hard decisions that come from putting Him first in all things. It's good to be as specific in your prayers as you can. Focus on the particular areas where you feel that your husband could grow with regard to looking to God and His viewpoint first. Also, mention areas where you feel he could grow in putting God first in his time, with his talents, and with your finances. Praise the Lord for those times when He asked you to sacrifice financially and you responded in faith and put His wishes first and denied yourself something that you really wanted. Encourage your husband when he wrestles through the tests that God sends to him to put the Lord first.

Praying for Blessing and Intervention

> Gracious Lord, the success of our home depends a great deal on how well my husband puts You first in his heart, mind, and soul. Help him to see the cause and effect relationship between his relationship with You and Your intervention and provision in our home, his career, our church, and his community impact. Give him practical ways to nourish and nurture his prioritization of Your will through a relational abiding with You. Provide him with friends who will also encourage and model for him what it means to put You first in every area of his life. Thank You, in Christ's name, amen.

17

Courage: Teachable Spirit

*"Whoever disregards discipline comes to poverty and shame,
but whoever heeds correction is honored"* (Proverbs 13:18).

Praising God

Heavenly Father, Your Word tells us in Proverbs 9:9, 'Instruct the wise and they will be wiser still; teach the righteous and they will add to their learning.' When my husband has a teachable spirit, he will be positioned and primed to grow even more with each experience in life. A foundation of humility leads to a teachable spirit, Lord. Undergird his mind and emotions with courage—courage not only in You but in who You have made him to be. That courage will give both humility and a teachable spirit the opportunity to flourish. Thank You for the confidence and courage You provide to all who look to You and trust You completely."

Presenting the Situation

Use this portion to bring to the Lord any concerns you may have regarding your husband's ability to possess a teachable spirit. If there are no concerns, then praise God for the development He has done in your husband's life in this area and for the favor shown to you for marrying a man with both humility and a teachable heart. If, however, your husband has an arrogant or prideful and demanding attitude, then you know God will be working deeply to break that stronghold and develop inner humility. Give your husband extra grace when God is busy reshaping him to be more like Christ, and intercede for him with the Lord.

Praying for Blessing and Intervention

Gracious Lord, fear, insecurity, and a need to feel in control can sometimes get in the way of the ability to learn from others and from You. I pray that You will give my husband a healthy amount of courage so that these things don't stand between him and his high calling of living with humility and a teachable heart. Let him understand that being teachable is an honorable way to live and reflects tremendous personal significance. Help him to see my respect for him when he does demonstrate humility and a teachable spirit. Help me never to withdraw my respect for him as my husband even when he demonstrates a lack of humility and courage, as we are all in process. Let my respect encourage him so that he longs to maintain that humble mind-set in all he does. In Christ's name, amen.

18

Community: Ministry Opportunities in the Church or Community

"Do not forget to do good and to share with others, for with such sacrifices God is pleased" (Hebrews 13:16).

Praising God

Heavenly Father, serving others provides an opportunity for my husband to reflect who You are to those around him. It also gives him the chance to become a greater recipient of Your blessings and favor as You flow through him to positively impact the lives of people in need. Thank You for the joy and satisfaction that You provide when we use the time, talents, and resources You've given us to make this world a better place. And thank You for the ways You have already provided for my husband so that he is in a position to use what You have given to him to help someone else."

Presenting the Situation

Use this portion to highlight any specific needs you may see around you that your husband could meet, whether through serving at the church or in your community. Ask God to reveal to you and him the particular place He wants your husband to minister. If your husband does not seem to have a great passion for ministry opportunities, ask God to ignite a desire in him in that direction. Share with your husband particular needs in the lives of the poor, orphans, sick, elderly, widows, and single mothers who come into your life and ask him if he would like for you or both of you to help.

Praying for Blessing and Intervention

Gracious Lord, even though life can get busy and the demands of family, work, and all else can weigh heavy on my husband's time and spirit, I ask that You give him insight into ways he can naturally serve You with the gifts and skills You've blessed him with. Help me to come alongside of him as an encourager and a helper so that he can experience great joy as we work for You together. God, please develop a heart of service in my husband and help him to recognize the importance of bettering other people's lives while also bringing You glory. Show him the specific place You want him to serve, whether at church or in the community, and please help him to be obedient to Your calling on his life in this area. Help me to be his greatest cheerleader and supporter when he serves the needs of others. In Christ's name, amen.

19

Courage: Stir Up the Dream Within Him

"The purposes of a person's heart are deep waters, but one who has insight draws them out" (Proverbs 20:5).

Praising God

Heavenly Father, I praise You and pray to You according to the prayer written for us in Psalm 90:17, which says, 'May the favor of the Lord our God rest on us; establish the work of our hands for us—yes, establish the work of our hands.' You are able to establish the work of my husband's hands and to stir up the dream within him. You are the Dream Giver and as such have placed the seed of the dream You desire him to fulfill within him. Thank You for the dream You've given him to live out. Thank You for all the dreams You've made for him to pursue, enjoy, and claim. I praise You, Dream Giver, for the hope of Your calling and the magnitude of what You have uniquely crafted my husband to accomplish."

Presenting the Situation

Use this portion to think back over past conversations you've had with your husband, times when he shared with you the things he was dreaming about doing one day. Also consider the things you've witnessed him passionately enjoy or pursue, including his hobbies. Oftentimes God links together people's passions, interests, background, skills, and desires and has them intersect at their dream. Take a moment to prayerfully cover all these areas of your husband's life, asking God to join them together and bring about the full manifestation of their culmination in carrying out God's dream and the dreams in your husband's life.

Praying for Blessing and Intervention

> Gracious Lord, stir up the dream within my husband's spirit, heart, and mind. Give him no rest until he embraces the pursuit of the dream You have given him at this point in his life to fulfill. Let him be filled with Your courage to take the necessary risk to push forward past the routine of Ordinary and into the Land of Extraordinary. Release him from the chains of his comfort zone and strengthen his resolve to move beyond any Border Bullies who discourage him with all their unbelief. I long to see my husband fulfilled, satisfied, and challenged as he accomplishes the dreams You've gifted him to live out. Grant me the desire of my heart to be a part of Your work in my husband's life as You bring about the life of his dreams. In Christ's name, amen.

20

Career: Flourish and Enjoy His Work

"This is what I have observed to be good: that it is appropriate for a person to eat, to drink and to find satisfaction in their toilsome labor under the sun during the few days of life God has given them—for this is their lot" (Ecclesiastes 5:18).

Praising God

Heavenly Father, You have instructed us that whatever we do, we are to work at it with all of our heart because we are ultimately working directly for You, not merely for a human boss or a paycheck or for our own feelings of significance (Colossians 3:23). This is the right mind-set to have with regard to our careers. Thank You for instructing my husband through Your Word on how he is to view his career. You are the originator of work itself because 'the Lord God took the man and put him in the Garden of Eden to work it and take care of it' (Genesis 2:15). My husband will gain the greatest satisfaction in his career when he views his work through the lens of serving You. He will also discover his greatest successes when he commits his career to You and the spreading of Your glory. You tell us in Proverbs 16:3, 'Commit to the Lord whatever you do, and he will establish your plans.' You will bring about that which is fully committed to You in love. Thank You for the assurance we have through Your promises as it relates to what is done in our work and career."

Presenting the Situation

Use this portion to pray specifically for your husband's satisfaction in his work. Ask God to bring a great amount of joy, pleasure, and fun to what he is doing for work. Look for ways where your husband may want to expand his skills and pray that those over him in authority will give him opportunities that will enable him to seek even greater success and satisfaction in his work. If your husband has not yet found a job that he enjoys or feels purposeful in doing, ask God to open doors for other jobs that may suit him more fully.

Praying for Blessing and Intervention

Gracious Lord, it is good to find satisfaction in our work. Your Word tells us that work is a blessing from You. I want my husband to be satisfied in what he is doing and to feel like he is making a significant contribution to others through his time, skills, and efforts. Help my husband to thoroughly enjoy his work. Thank You for the income that it provides for us as a family, but beyond the income, let it also provide an increase in energy, purpose, and meaning that overflows onto all members of our home. If my husband is not in the line of work that You have planned and created him to do, then please arrange and rearrange things in our lives so that he will be willing and able to walk through new doors of opportunity when You bring them his way. In Christ's name, amen.

21

Character: Protection from Immoral Relationships and Pornography

*"Marriage should be honored by all, and the marriage
bed kept pure, for God will judge the adulterer
and all the sexually immoral"* (Hebrews 13:4).

Praising God

Heavenly Father, the instructions You've given us in the area of morality and relationships with others are very clear. You tell us, 'Above all else, guard your heart, for everything you do flows from it' (Proverbs 4:23). You also make it clear that we are to 'flee from sexual immorality. All other sins a person commits are outside the body, but whoever sins sexually, sins against their own body' (1 Corinthians 6:18). You could not have made Your wisdom and instruction any clearer. It is in following Your commands for holy living that my husband (and our entire family, by virtue of his obedience) will experience the full blessing of Your peace, protection, and power. Thank You for giving us Your truth to guide us as well as the Holy Spirit to strengthen us against temptation and immorality."

Presenting the Situation

Use this portion to ask God to cultivate in you the qualities of love found in 1 Corinthians 13:4-7. These qualities include patience, kindness, acquiescence, and the ability to keep no record of wrong and not to be easily angered. Love also does not delight in evil but rejoices in truth. Love always protects, trusts, hopes, and endures. In your marriage, you are responsible for you and not your husband. When suspicion or jealousy arise in a spouse's heart, it leads to a division of love because neither of those things are found in authentic love. Rather than focusing on any suspicions, ask God to help you focus on cultivating a heart that purely loves your husband and rests in the reality that your trust is ultimately in God and His sovereign ability to intervene, redirect, and protect your husband from falling into any immorality.

Praying for Blessing and Intervention

Gracious Lord, there are things in my husband's life that are outside of my control that can cause me anxiety, fear, and pain. Some of these things include suspicions I may have or jealousies that may arise in me concerning my husband. Whether these are founded in truth or not, I repent of my emotional reactions to these thoughts and ask that You will align my heart in a spirit of biblical love and trust. I ask that You station Your angels around my husband to protect him from any immoral advances or temptations from friends, co-workers, or women he meets. Give his spirit a special sensitivity to be on the alert against straying morally through an illicit emotional or physical relationship, or through pornography of all types. Help us both to satisfy each other in the areas of romance and sexual intimacy, fully, deeply, and completely. In Christ's name, amen.

Career: Traveling Mercies

"It is written, 'He will command his angels concerning you to guard you carefully'" (Luke 4:10).

Praising God

Heavenly Father, 'Surely, LORD, you bless the righteous; you surround them with your favor as with a shield' (Psalm 5:12). You are my husband's protection when he travels, whether he's traveling for work or pleasure. Because I trust in You, I release the worry and anxiety I feel as he travels, knowing that You watch over him and that his safety and protection are found in You. As the psalmist writes, 'No harm will overtake you, no disaster will come near your tent. For he will command his angels concerning you to guard you in all your ways; they will lift you up in their hands, so that you will not strike your foot against a stone' (Psalm 91:10-12). And also, 'The LORD will keep you from all harm—he will watch over your life; the LORD will watch over your coming and going both now and forevermore' (Psalm 121:7-8). Thank You for the assurance of Your Word and Your promises that I can claim in my prayers for my husband's safety and traveling mercies, and help me to rest in peace rather than worry."

Presenting the Situation

Use this portion to list any upcoming trips your husband has planned or may plan. Also include his commute to and from work, and any family outings or trips you have scheduled. God delights to hear about the daily details of our lives. Let Him know that you are looking to Him for traveling mercies in each of these areas and make this a regular part of your daily prayers, updating the requests with the new travel plans.

Praying for Blessing and Intervention

Gracious Lord, please surround my husband with Your presence as he travels. Let Your angels stand guard not only around our family members while we are home but also while my husband travels—either long distance or short. Lead me away from a spirit of concern and give me the grace to rest in the confidence of Your protection. You see all, know all, and are involved in all that happens, so I look to You as our loving protector in every way. Help my husband not only to be safe as he travels but also help his travels to always go smoothly, whether it's a plane connection, traffic, or any other thing that could prove to be frustrating to him. I ask that You go before him and behind him, making his way smooth so that he returns to us with his energies high and his spirit refreshed. Thank You, Lord, in Christ's name, amen.

23

Career: Eternal Perspective

*"…into an inheritance that can never perish, spoil, or fade.
This inheritance is kept in heaven for you"* (1 Peter 1:4).

Praising God

Heavenly Father, thank You for the many ways You've equipped my husband for the work that he does. Thank You for the skills, gifts, insight, and character You've developed in him to be employed and perform his work well. His work is valuable not only to him but also to us as a family. But, God, You have also reminded us in Your Word to keep an eternal mind-set so that we are not only working for tangible benefits on earth but also for an eternal inheritance. It says in 1 Peter 1:3-4, 'Praise be to the God and Father of our Lord Jesus Christ! In his great mercy he has given us new birth into a living hope through the resurrection of Jesus Christ from the dead, and into an inheritance that can never perish, spoil or fade. This inheritance is kept in heaven for you.' Thank You for the opportunity to increase our inheritance in heaven based on what is done on earth for Your glory and kingdom."

Presenting the Situation

Use this portion to talk to God about any specific situations you are aware of regarding your husband's work that could use God's intervention. In the areas where you have witnessed an eternal mind-set influence your husband's thoughts regarding work, thank God for them. Ask Him to develop an even greater eternal perspective in your family, your marriage, and your husband's view toward his own work as well as yours. Look for ways you complement each other and can work together to bring about eternal benefit in the lives of others.

Praying for Blessing and Intervention

Gracious Lord, open my husband's eyes and heart to truly understand the eternal consequences of the choices he makes in this life. Cultivate in him a desire to store up treasures in heaven, where neither moth nor rust will destroy them. Help my words and conversations with him to be seasoned in such a way that encourages him to fully adopt an eternal mind-set with regard to his work, and life in general. Show us how best to serve You with our time, talents, and resources. Thank You that You bless us with an abundance of joy when we do seek to use what You have entrusted to each of us for an eternal impact. Thank You God for giving us this time on earth to prepare for eternity. In Christ's name, amen.

24

Career: Favor on the Job

"May the favor of the Lord our God rest on us;
establish the work of our hands for us—yes,
establish the work of our hands" (Psalm 90:17).

Praising God

Heavenly Father, thank You for the work You have given to my husband. Favor carries with it so many blessings that I pray first and foremost that You will give him Your abundant favor. In summarizing the prayer of Jabez, 'Bless my husband, indeed. Place Your hand of favor upon him, and expand his borders. Keep him from evil that he might not experience or cause pain' (see 1 Chronicles 4:10); 'The LORD bless [him] and keep [him]; the LORD make his face shine on [him] and be gracious to [him]; the LORD turn his face toward [him] and give [him] peace' (Numbers 6:24-26). I pray that You bless my husband abundantly by giving him favor with those he works under, for, and around so that in all things at all times, having all that he needs, he will abound in every good work (2 Corinthians 9:8). Thank You for Your treasured favor, Lord, and for Your gift of stimulating others to show favor toward my husband in his work."

Presenting the Situation

Use this portion to mention the people your husband works under, for, and with by name and ask God to give your husband favor with each of them. Seek God's favor on the things your husband does at work, whether it's projects or ideas he has. Ask your husband to share with you the key areas where he specifically seeks the blessing of God. Ask God to open those doors for him through favor that he would not have been able to open on his own.

Praying for Blessing and Intervention

Gracious Lord, surround my husband with Your favor as a shield. Let kindness overflow into the hearts and minds of those he works with. Give him favor for the ideas and concepts he brings to the table. Give him favor with the people he works with and the people he comes across during his work, Lord. Let him walk in confidence, knowing that I am praying for him and that He has your favor in and on his life. Give him wit, grace, and a charisma that endears him to others in such a way that causes his work to be even more fruitful than it would be without those qualities. Bless the work of his hands in all that he does and let him find satisfaction and fulfillment in that which You've called him to do. If You desire for him to shift into a different role or line of work, I ask that You guide his heart and open doors of favor in the direction You have for him. In Christ's name, amen.

25

Communication: Listening to God's Guidance

"I will instruct you and teach you in the way which you should go; I will counsel you with my loving eye upon you" (Psalm 32:8).

Praising God

Heavenly Father, the Word of God and our prayers are Your pathways to communicating with You and sensing Your precious guidance. Thank You for telling us in Jeremiah 33:3, 'Call to me and I will answer you and tell you great and unsearchable things you do not know.' The guidance and direction that my husband needs can be found when he talks to You and learns how to wait on You in order to discern Your wisdom and direction. I desire for my husband to lead and guide our family according to Your will; knowing that Your Spirit is leading and guiding him brings me great peace. Align our hearts with Your will so that we can live as 1 John 5:14 says, 'This is the confidence we have in approaching God: that if we ask anything according to his will, he hears us.' I praise You for Your willingness to hear us in prayer."

Presenting the Situation

Use this portion to talk to the Lord about certain areas of your husband's life, your marriage, or your family that you feel need God's guidance at this time in particular. Be specific in listing the areas where you need the Lord's wisdom. Spend some time asking for God's wisdom to be given to your husband for each of these. And ask that God will prepare your heart to follow his lead once he has heard from the Lord concerning the situations you are praying about.

Praying for Blessing and Intervention

Gracious Lord, Your Word says that if any of us lacks wisdom, we can ask You and You will give it freely. I ask that You supply my husband with Your wisdom on each and every decision he needs to make for himself and for our family. Increase his hunger to know You and to seek Your wisdom himself. Give me a gentle spirit that responds to his leadership, coupled with an unwavering trust in You to work through him. Guide my husband's thoughts, words, and actions, Lord. And give him a heart and a spirit that are receptive to Your leading. In Christ's name, amen.

26

Courage: Spiritual Leader of the Home

"These commandments that I give you today are to be on your hearts. Impress them on your children. Talk about them when you sit at home and when you walk along the road, when you lie down and when you get up" (Deuteronomy 6:6-7).

Praising God

Heavenly Father, You have created an order for the home through which Your glory, power, and favor flow. This order is written for us in 1 Corinthians 11:3, which says, 'But I want you to realize that the head of every man is Christ, and the head of the woman is man, and the head of Christ is God.' To begin, my husband is under Christ and is accountable to submit and surrender to the will of Christ in all that he does. Then I am to be under my husband in submission to the spiritual leadership he brings to us under Christ. This does not negate equality, as we are both equal and have full access to You, Lord, but it does refer to spiritual leadership. Help my husband to rise to the occasion of the spiritual leader in our home and follow the words of Deuteronomy 6:4-9: 'Hear, O Israel: The LORD our

God, the LORD is one. Love the LORD your God with all your heart and with all your soul and with all your strength. These commandments that I give you today are to be on your hearts. Impress them on your children. Talk about them when you sit at home and when you walk along the road, when you lie down and when you get up. Tie them as symbols on your hands and bind them on your foreheads. Write them on the doorframes of your houses and on your gates.'"

Presenting the Situation

Use this portion to thank the Lord for those specific situations when your husband has demonstrated spiritual leadership in your home. Thank Him for these times and share with God how that makes you feel to be underneath your husband's spiritual leadership. Ask God to strengthen particular weak areas in your husband's character, motivation, and heart that would enable him to take greater initiative in living out the role of spiritual leader in your family and marriage.

Praying for Blessing and Intervention

Gracious Lord, bless my husband with the courage to be the spiritual leader in our home. Strengthen his resolve to fill these shoes consistently and with a spirit of compassion toward those he leads, especially me. I ask that You increase in him the desire to witness me growing spiritually and that he will seek to invest in things (whether it's time, conferences, or resources) that will help us both develop in spiritual maturity and personal discipleship. Give me a gentle and receptive spirit in response to his leadership, and I pray that You will embolden him to live out the full biblical description of what a husband should be. Light the flame in his heart for You, Lord, so that he looks to You in all things. And give him a graceful humility that allows him to submit himself underneath the Lordship of Jesus Christ. As he surrenders to You, I find increased freedom and rest to submit and surrender to his leadership. In Christ's name, amen.

27

Character:
Financial Stewardship

*"Each of you should give what you have decided in your
heart to give, not reluctantly or under compulsion, for
God loves a cheerful giver"* (2 Corinthians 9:7).

Praising God

Heavenly Father, Your viewpoint on our finances is much
different from the world's focus on accumulating things
and providing for our pleasures. I desire for my husband to align
his thoughts with Yours so that our marriage and our home can
experience the blessings of Your provision. As it says in Luke
6:38, 'Give, and it will be given to you. A good measure, pressed
down, shaken together and running over, will be poured into
your lap. For with the measure you use, it will be measured to
you.' You will return to us whatever is given because no one can
out-give You, Lord. You say in Malachi 3:10, '"Bring the whole
tithe into the storehouse, that there may be food in my house.
Test me in this," says the LORD Almighty, "and see if I will not
throw open the floodgates of heaven and pour out so much
blessing that there will not be room enough to store it."' Also
in Luke 12:15, 'Then he said to them, "Watch out! Be on your

guard against all kinds of greed; life does not consist in an abundance of possessions.'" Thank You for Your Word that guides and instructs us on how to live obediently with our finances."

Presenting the Situation

Use this portion to bring your financial details before the Lord in prayer. If you have debt, let God know you are seeking to find a way to pay it off and free yourself from financial liabilities in the future. Mention the specific debt you have and ask Him how to change the use of your finances to pay it off efficiently. Also tell God thank You for the ways your husband has stewarded your finances well in the past or present, mentioning different scenarios where you have witnessed this.

Praying for Blessing and Intervention

Gracious Lord, develop in my husband a deep desire to honor You first and foremost with our finances. Help him to see the reward that comes by giving to You and giving to others in Your name. You say in the Proverbs that "whoever is kind to the poor lends to the LORD, and he will reward them for what they have done" (19:17). Open my husband's heart so that he will want to help those in need more than we already do. And give both of us restraint so that we don't overspend on possessions, vacations, or diversions. Help us to establish a savings fund (or grow an existing one) and maintain it at a healthy level. Thank You, God. In Christ's name, amen.

28

Communication: Handling Disagreements

"A gentle answer turns away wrath, but a harsh word stirs up anger" (Proverbs 15:1).

Praising God

Heavenly Father, disagreements are bound to happen in our relationship. Conflict is a normal part of being human. Rather than pray to avoid disagreements, God, I ask that You equip us to handle our disagreements with honor and respect for each other. Help our marriage to reflect Your instruction found in Ephesians 4:29-32: 'Do not let any unwholesome talk come out of your mouths, but only what is helpful for building others up according to their needs, that it may benefit those who listen. And do not grieve the Holy Spirit of God, with whom you were sealed for the day of redemption. Get rid of all bitterness, rage and anger, brawling and slander, along with every form of malice. Be kind and compassionate to one another, forgiving each other, just as in Christ God forgave you.' I praise You for giving us the blueprint for how to communicate in our marriage and in our home so that You are always pleased."

Presenting the Situation

Use this portion to repent of any times you have spoken harshly to your husband or have used critical tones or words. Examine any times he may have hurt you when you had a disagreement or faced conflict. Ask the Lord to help you forgive one another. Then ask God to infiltrate your thoughts and words so that they are pleasing to Him, even in the midst of conflict.

Praying for Blessing and Intervention

Gracious Lord, let the words of my mouth and the words of my husband's mouth bring life to each other rather than death. Words are powerful and so are our tone and body language. I ask that You give us examples in the lives of godly couples to see what healthy communication in the midst of conflict is to look like, especially if we have not witnessed it before. Please help us not to shut down or run from disagreements either. You tell us not to let the sun set on our anger, so please give us a willingness on both our parts to resolve our disagreements in a timely, respectful, and kind manner. In Christ's name, amen.

29

Communion: Reading and Meditating on God's Word

"Keep this Book of the Law always on your lips; meditate on it day and night, so that you may be careful to do everything written in it. Then you will be prosperous and successful" (Joshua 1:8).

Praising God

Heavenly Father, Your Word is my husband's guide for all of the decisions he needs to make in his life. Many of these decisions impact me and our family and even our future. You instruct us in Joshua 1:8 concerning Your Word, 'Keep this Book of the Law always on your lips; meditate on it day and night, so that you may be careful to do everything written in it. Then you will be prosperous and successful.' When he keeps Your Word in his heart and meditates on it, it will enable him to make choices that reflect Your will. In that way, his choices will be successful in Your sight. I praise You for providing Your Word that enables us to achieve success, joy, and contentment together."

Presenting the Situation

Use this portion to talk to God about the ways you've witnessed your husband use God's Word in decision making, or the times you've experienced your husband's hunger for Scripture. Thank God for these situations. Then spend some time asking God to intervene in your husband's schedule and open up greater opportunities for engaging with God's Word and bringing His truth to bear on your marriage and home life.

Praying for Blessing and Intervention

Gracious Lord, I ask that You increase the hunger in my husband to know Your Word and to meditate and reflect on it. Give him a desire to understand Your thoughts and Your character. Help him to find resources that guide him to a deeper understanding of Scripture and open up windows of time where he can naturally incorporate the reading of or meditating on Your Word into his life. I pray that You make me a model of what it means to daily reflect on Your Word and apply Your principles in my life. Let that stimulate him to increase his time with You, God, and grow in his knowledge, understanding, and application of what You say (Ezra 7:10). In Christ's name, amen.

30

Communion: Abiding Relationship with Christ

"If you remain in me and my words remain in you, ask whatever you wish, and it will be done for you" (John 15:7).

Praising God

Heavenly Father, my husband's relationship with Jesus Christ is the source of his well-being, wisdom, strength, and peace. You have established life in this way and tell us in John 15:4, 'Remain in me, as I also remain in you. No branch can bear fruit by itself; it must remain in the vine. Neither can you bear fruit unless you remain in me.' Enable my husband to get a taste of what it truly means to abide in Christ, at a level beyond what he has ever known before. Help him live out Galatians 2:20, which says, 'I have been crucified with Christ and I no longer live, but Christ lives in me. The life I now live in the body, I live by faith in the Son of God, who loved me and gave himself for me.' It is in maintaining an abiding walk with Christ that he will fully experience the manifestation of his destiny and purpose in life and give You glory."

Presenting the Situation

Use this portion to tell God the ways in which you've witnessed your husband's abiding fellowship with Jesus Christ and to thank Him for them. Then spend the remaining time in this section of prayer focusing on the specific areas where you would like to see your husband grow in his abiding relationship with Christ.

Praying for Blessing and Intervention

Gracious Lord, only in an intimate, abiding fellowship with Christ will my husband find the strength and wisdom he needs to lead our marriage and home and to carry out his purpose through the community and church activities, as well as in his work in the marketplace. Yet abiding with Christ requires a level of attunement and alignment that is often beyond what we may currently understand and accomplish on our own. It also often requires a fellowship with Christ's sufferings to taste His humility. I pray for Your gentle favor in encouraging my husband to increase his sweet fellowship with You. I pray that he will know Jesus personally as You draw him to You so that he can walk in Your ways. Let him be so excited about his relationship with Jesus that he seeks to share the same development of maturity with me and the others in our family. I pray that this abiding presence will also equip him to carry out the good works that You have prepared for him to live out all the days of his life. In Christ's name, amen.

31

Confession: Repenting of Sins

"Do you show contempt for the riches of his
kindness, forbearance and patience, not
realizing that God's kindness is intended to
lead you to repentance?" (Romans 2:4).

Praising God

Heavenly Father, You tell us in 1 John 1:9 that if we confess our sins, You are faithful and just and will forgive us our sins and purify us from all unrighteousness. Your forgiveness is as close as a prayer of repentance and confession. But the repentance that precedes that prayer needs to be coupled with godly sorrow, a sorrow that leaves no regret (2 Corinthians 7:10). Thank You for removing the sting of sin and the guilt of regret when repentance is done according to Your prescribed fashion. I praise You for having the heart that gives us a new beginning time and time again, and allows us to build on the solid foundation of forgiveness in our marriage and our home."

Presenting the Situation

Use this portion to talk to God about any specific situations in your husband's life that you may have insight into where he needs to repent. You might not be certain or just have a suspicion about certain things, but God knows the reality he faces, so present your requests to God as specifically as you can, couched in grace that gives your husband the benefit of the doubt. Ask God to draw your husband to repentance in these areas, but to do it through His kindness. Pray a hedge of protection around your husband during the process of being brought to repentance since the vulnerability of repenting can open the door for guilt, regret, and depression to seep in instead of the joy of the Lord's restoration.

Praying for Blessing and Intervention

> Gracious Lord, draw my husband to You with Your kindness. Bring Him to repentance, but do so with Your mercy. Please open his heart and cause him to be sensitive to Your leading and the Holy Spirit's conviction in his life regarding sins he is currently involved in or sins from the past that he has not yet repented of. Show him the freedom that he can know through Your forgiveness and give me a heart to forgive him where he has sinned against me as well. For those sins we have committed together, please lead us both to repentance before You and bless us with Your peace, joy, and hope, knowing that we are fully forgiven and can boldly approach You in prayer about anything we may need. In Christ's name, amen.

32

Communion: Having the Mind of Christ

"'Who has known the mind of the Lord so as to instruct him?' But we have the mind of Christ" (1 Corinthians 2:16).

Praising God

Heavenly Father, much of what makes up our lists of what we are to do and what we are not to do comes through man-made regulations. Even if the intention of these rules is well-meaning, they are birthed and based in a spirit of legalism rather than in the mind of Christ. As Your Word states in Colossians 2:23, 'Such regulations indeed have an appearance of wisdom, with their self-imposed worship, their false humility and their harsh treatment of the body, but they lack any value in restraining sensual indulgence.' These regulations may look like they can keep us from going down the wrong path, but that is an illusion. It is only in communing with You and living with the mind of Christ Himself as the dominant influence of our hearts and our thoughts that we discover the freedom of right living. Thank You for Your Word that tells us the secret to abundant life, found in Romans 8:6: 'The mind governed by the flesh is death, but the mind governed by the Spirit is life and peace.' Thank You for giving my husband the opportunity to live his life governed by Your Spirit through abiding with Jesus Christ and being instructed by Your Word."

Presenting the Situation

Use this portion to share with God about any concerns you may have in how your husband makes his decisions. If there is any hint of legalism in him or in your relationship, take these issues to the Lord and ask God to reveal His abundant grace and wisdom to you both. Look for specific situations you can talk to God about regarding your husband's line of thinking, choices, and even his belief system. Seek God's power in drawing your husband to Him so that his mind is governed by the Spirit and the Word and so that he lives in harmony with the mind of Christ.

Praying for Blessing and Intervention

Gracious Lord, break the bonds of legalism that influence our thoughts and our home, and show us where and how legalistic thinking may be impacting us in ways we are not even yet aware. True power and restraint from unrighteousness come only through having the mind of Christ and surrendering to the Spirit's rule in our hearts. Please help my husband to value his time with You, whether that is in formal occasions of devotion or scattered moments throughout his day. Give him a keen discernment to know what is of You and what is merely carnal thinking. Help him to lead our home with grace, dignity, and tenderness. In Christ's name, amen.

33

Community: Godly Male Friends and Mentors

"Perfume and incense bring joy to the heart, and the pleasantness of a friend springs from their heartfelt advice" (Proverbs 27:9).

Praising God

Heavenly Father, 'as iron sharpens iron, so one person sharpens another' (Proverbs 27:17), please send godly mentors and friends to my husband. You have placed us on earth in the context of community because it is our interaction with each other that promotes our growth and helps to develop our character. As Your Word says in 1 Thessalonians 5:11, 'Therefore encourage one another and build each other up, just as in fact you are doing.' I praise You for the wisdom of relationships and thank You for the godly men You have put in my husband's relational circle throughout his life. Please deepen these relationships and bring more spiritual men to him in order to mentor him into a person who exhibits Christ's character in all he does."

Presenting the Situation

Use this portion to thank God specifically for any godly friends that your husband has or has had over the course of his life. These can also include family members. Ask God to bless these men and enrich their lives because of the impact they've had in your husband's life. If your husband has not had many godly male friends, ask God to bring a couple of them into his life and to cause your husband's heart to be open to receiving them. Also ask God to open your heart to sharing your husband with them.

Praying for Blessing and Intervention

> Gracious Lord, please surround my husband with men and mentors who guide him in the ways of wisdom, right living, kindness, commitment, and a deep love for You and for his family. I pray that You bless him with like interests with these men and provide them with learning experiences that they can share together, as well as occasions of fun and fellowship. Help me to be willing to share my husband's emotions and time so that he can develop and sustain relationships with these men, and I pray that the richness of their relationships will overflow into our marriage and into our home. In Christ's name, amen.

34

Career: Protection Physically, Emotionally, and Spiritually

"Surely he will save you from the fowler's snare and from the deadly pestilence. He will cover you with his feathers, and under his wings you will find refuge; his faithfulness will be your shield and rampart" (Psalm 91:3-4).

Praising God

Heavenly Father, You are our refuge and strength, an ever-present help in trouble (Psalm 46:1). My husband's safety—whether that be physical protection, emotional security, or spiritual covering—comes directly from You. As Your Word says in 1 John 5:18, 'We know that anyone born of God does not continue to sin; the One who was born of God keeps them safe, and the evil one cannot harm them.' You are even my husband's protection from sin itself and temptation. Thank You for the instruction of Your Word and the peace that comes in knowing I can look to You with my worries, concerns, and fears about my husband and our family's protection."

Presenting the Situation

Use this portion to talk to God about any specific trips coming up that your husband may be taking or you may be taking as a family. Also share with God any areas of concern or anxiety you have when he travels. Look beyond the areas of physical safety to include areas that you want God to cover your husband spiritually and emotionally. It could be with regard to sin's temptation or simply emotional and physical exhaustion. Be as specific as possible in asking God to protect your husband from the many dangers and snares that the enemy seeks to put in his path.

Praying for Blessing and Intervention

> Gracious Lord, be to my husband a shield and a strong tower, covering him with the protection and security he needs to fully live out and accomplish the destiny You have created him for. Relieve my worry and anxiety regarding his health, emotional purity, spiritual fervor, and physical safety. Let us both look to You as our guard, asking that You station Your angels around our home and our cars and our hearts, guiding us away from potential danger and toward security and peace. Thank You for Your presence and for Your willingness to answer our prayers. In Christ's name, amen.

35

Courage: Increase His Faith

"Now faith is confidence in what we hope for and
assurance about what we do not see" (Hebrews 11:1).

Praising God

Heavenly Father, we read in Matthew 21:22, 'If you believe, you will receive whatever you ask for in prayer.' Belief is the foundation of faith. When my husband's belief rests in You and the reality that he can do all things through You, who gives him strength (Philippians 4:13), his faith will enable him to fulfill the dreams You have planted in his heart as the Dream Giver. Your apostles said to Jesus, 'Increase our faith!' in Luke 17:5, and so I intercede gratefully on behalf of my husband to ask You to increase the depth and breadth of his faith as well. I desire for him to live out his destiny, Lord, and Mark 9:23 tells us that 'everything is possible for one who believes.' I praise You for the power of faith. May that power embolden my husband to make decisions rooted in courage, to break through the Border Bullies that loom to intimidate and delay him from pursuing his dreams."

Presenting the Situation

Use this portion to speak with God about specific areas of

your husband's current situations in life where you feel he could benefit from increased faith and courage. Mention these situations by name and ask God to intervene in response to your authentic and heartfelt prayer on behalf of your husband. Also ask God to open your heart and reveal to you any areas in your husband's spiritual life where he may lack boldness and faith so that you can cover those areas with prayer and shower him with your encouragement.

Praying for Blessing and Intervention

Gracious Lord, make me an instrument of encouragement in my husband's life. Let my words always be used to build up and not tear down. When he allows himself to be vulnerable and shares his fears with me, I pray that I will honor those moments and conversations with a listening and understanding ear. Encouragement is stronger than empathy, God, so teach me the skills I need to bring consistent encouragement into my husband's life in the areas where his faith needs to grow and develop. Strengthen my own faith as well so that I can be a witness and testimony to Your power and to the power of faith and believing in You. In Christ's name, amen.

36

Courage: Pure Heart

"Blessed are the pure in heart, for they
will see God" (Matthew 5:8).

Praising God

Heavenly Father, blessed are the pure in heart, for they will see You (Matthew 5:8). A pure heart opens the pathway to Your presence and the flow of Your purpose in our lives. You tell us in 2 Timothy 2:22, 'Flee the evil desires of youth and pursue righteousness, faith, love and peace, along with those who call on the Lord out of a pure heart.' And in 1 John 3:3, 'All who have this hope in him purify themselves, just as he is pure.' I praise You for Your holiness and Your purity, without which none of us could withstand the fullness of Your holy judgment apart from the saving sacrifice of Jesus Christ. In return, You call us to a life of purity, and I thank You that my husband is on the path of purity and that You will enable his heart to continue to develop in this character quality."

Presenting the Situation

Use this portion to confess any known sin that you may have participated in with your husband before or since you were married. Ask the Lord to convict your husband with any attitudes or actions of unrighteousness. Talk to the Lord about specific situations where you need to forgive your husband and any areas that you need to ask him for forgiveness. Ask God to give you both the grace to do so. Through forgiveness, freedom is found and love is rekindled.

Praying for Blessing and Intervention

Gracious Lord, create in my husband a clean and pure heart. Let his thoughts and words honor You and respect and honor our marriage. Guard his motivations for success and greatness so that they remain rooted in humility, in service, and in You. Give him the courage to repent of his sins and turn from them. I pray that any hidden sins will be brought to light by Your grace and power. Bring about the purifying of his heart in all things. In Christ's name, amen.

37

Courage: Facing Problems and Challenges

"The God of all grace, who called you to his eternal glory in Christ, after you have suffered a little while, will himself restore you and make you strong, firm and steadfast" (1 Peter 5:10).

Praising God

Heavenly Father, I praise You that through You my husband can be 'strengthened with all power according to [Your] glorious might so that [he] may have great endurance and patience' (Colossians 1:11). You are 'a refuge for the oppressed, a stronghold in times of trouble. Those who know your name trust in you, for you, LORD, have never forsaken those who seek you' (Psalm 9:9-10). Remind me to look to You when my husband faces problems or challenges that I feel unable to help solve. Remind me to put my faith, hope, and trust in You and to go to You on his behalf to intercede for him against the trials of life that seek to discourage and defeat him."

Presenting the Situation

Use this portion to pray about any problems or challenges that you are aware of that your husband is facing right now.

Spend some time mentioning these issues by name and asking God to provide the power, wisdom, and courage to your husband at such a deep level that he will literally feel your prayers on his behalf. Ask your husband to share any difficulties at work that he wishes could be solved with his boss or his co-workers. Ask him if there are any goals that his boss has laid out for him to achieve or that he has set for himself that need prayer. Also bring to the Lord any problems or challenges that you are facing together as a couple or with your children and grandchildren, and ask for God's favor and His grace to provide a pathway to peace and overcoming.

Praying for Blessing and Intervention

> Gracious Lord, give my husband a supernatural infusion of courage so that fear, anxiety, restlessness, and doubt do not hold him back from leading our family and chasing the dream You have planted in him. Help him to face the problems that come his and our way with the ability to work toward the solution, rather than become caught up in the troubling and negative emotions and responses that can naturally arise out of these difficult issues. Please open up our communication with each other so that we are able to truly understand each other and so that we don't create more problems on top of the ones that already exist. Remind us of the importance of facing challenges as a team, supporting each other through encouragement, patience, and tenderness. In Christ's name, amen.

38

Character: Loyalty

*"Let love and faithfulness never leave you; bind
them around your neck, write them on the
tablet of your heart"* (Proverbs 3:3).

Praising God

Heavenly Father, loyalty is Your hallmark. It is one of the
distinguishing facets of Your loving-kindness. Guide us
to be loyal to You, especially in seasons when we undergo difficult tests and trials. Father, You have written in Proverbs 3:3,
'Let love and faithfulness never leave you; bind them around
your neck, write them on the tablet of your heart.' You also
tell us that 'he who pursues righteousness and loyalty finds life,
righteousness and honor' (Proverbs 21:21 NASB). God, I pray
that loyalty to You will be a quality my husband possesses fully
and wholly, especially at those times when he may not feel
like being loyal, in those times when our closeness as a couple
may be lacking, or when we may be arguing. I look to You as
the model of loyalty, praising You that You have planted this
seed within our new nature, giving us both the opportunity to
grow and develop loyalty with unbroken loving-kindness in
all situations."

Presenting the Situation

Use this portion to talk with God about any fears, doubts, or feelings you may have concerning your husband's loyalty to God or to you. Name specific people you are concerned about or certain things you feel may be pulling his loyalty from you, whether that's work, a hobby, or even service to others. Ask God for clarity in your own thinking so that you model the definition of an ever-trusting love. Look to God to protect your marriage intimacy and depth of relationship.

Praying for Blessing and Intervention

Gracious Lord, forgive me for my fears and suspicions concerning my husband's heart. You've instructed me in Your Word that love always trusts and yet I lack trust from time to time. Cleanse my heart and help me to put my trust ultimately in You because I don't want to stand in Your way of intervening in my marriage to keep us dedicated to and devoted toward each other. Convict my husband of anything he may be entertaining or doing that would break his loyalty to me. Protect him with a shield around his heart, Lord. Enable me to meet his needs and satisfy him relationally and sexually. Cultivate in him a protective spirit around our relationship so that he desires to keep us strong as a couple and to draw near to me in all ways. In Christ's name, amen.

39

Character: Direct His Attention to You and Away from Inappropriate Entertainment

"Do not set foot on the path of the wicked or walk in the way of evildoers" (Proverbs 4:14).

Praising God

Heavenly Father, You give to each of us the continual invitation to draw near to You. I praise You that You have not chosen to dwell among the high and lofty but rather choose to spend Your time with people like us. James 4:8 instructs us, 'Come near to God and he will come near to you. Wash your hands, you sinners, and purify your hearts, you double-minded.' Coming near to You includes turning away from other things that seek to gain our attention such as inappropriate television programs or movies, YouTube videos, or any number of things. These things keep us from following the command in James 4:8. Thank You for calling us to purify our hearts before You."

Presenting the Situation

Use this portion to bring up any situations or distractions you recognize in your life and your husband's life that may be drawing you both away from God, rather than nearer to Him. Confess these things one by one, asking God to help you withdraw from each and every one of them. Thank God for how you have witnessed your husband drawing near to God and for the choices you have seen him make to turn down worldly entertainment or distractions in an effort to protect and preserve the purity of his heart and family.

Praying for Blessing and Intervention

> Gracious Lord, draw my husband's heart, spirit, and mind toward You with sincere affection and humility. Let Your goodness and kindness attract his attention. While I want him to have fun and enjoy life, I also ask that You protect him and draw him away from inappropriate entertainment, whether that is movies, TV shows, YouTube videos, or anything else. Please grant my husband self-control so he does not watch too much television and be too involved in Internet media. Please increase his personal restraint, Lord. Help me to be an encourager to my husband of what habits of holiness look like in my use of all media. Help him to see You through and in me and make me even more attractive to him. In Christ's name, amen.

40

Character: Taking Every Thought Captive

"You will keep in perfect peace those whose minds are steadfast, because they trust in you" (Isaiah 26:3).

Praising God

Heavenly Father, You have created us with a great deal of freedom in our thoughts. With our thoughts, we can promote peace in our lives and in our relationships. But our thoughts can drift into the negative and harmful, creating issues such as anxiety, fear, or frustration. You have supplied us an answer based on 2 Corinthians 10:5, which says, 'We demolish arguments and every pretension that sets itself up against the knowledge of God, and we take captive every thought to make it obedient to Christ.' Taking our thoughts captive enables us to keep our minds set on that which produces life, hope, and peace. I thank You and praise You for giving us a way to manage our thoughts to Your joy and our benefit."

Presenting the Situation

Use this portion to share with God any subjects or issues that you feel result from cultivating negative thinking or allowing worldly thoughts to germinate and remain in your husband's thoughts, and in yours. Ask God to set up a barrier against these types of thoughts and to give you both wisdom on how to feed your mind with positive and uplifting thoughts that don't hinder His will in your marriage and in your lives.

Praying for Blessing and Intervention

Gracious Lord, our troubles often stem from a lack of taking every thought captive to the obedience of Jesus Christ. Please forgive us both for allowing unguarded thoughts to take root. Give us gentle reminders throughout our day to direct our thoughts toward the truth of Christ, letting go of those things that are worldly, carnal, or fruitless. Give my husband self-restraint and insight to align his thoughts with Yours, letting go of those that do not bring You glory. Make me an encouragement to him, and keep me from criticizing him when I witness something that is not in alignment with You. Rather, let me turn my concern to You in prayer, trusting that You will bring about a resolution because of my faith in You. In Christ's name, amen.

41

Courage: Cultivating Certainty

"When you ask, you must believe and not doubt,
because the one who doubts is like a wave of the
sea, blown and tossed by the wind" (James 1:6).

Praising God

Heavenly Father, certainty is the bedrock of peace. It is the foundation of faith. It is the unshakable confidence that enables my husband to lead with security and assurance. Throughout Your Word, You have given us many people who modeled the grace of certainty. We read in Job 19:25, 'I know that my redeemer lives, and that in the end he will stand on the earth.' Also in Psalm 27:3, 'Though an army besiege me, my heart will not fear; though war break out against me, even then I will be confident.' And in Joshua 23:14, 'Now I am about to go the way of all the earth. You know with all your heart and soul that not one of all the good promises the LORD your God gave you has failed. Every promise has been fulfilled; not one has failed.' Those who served You well somehow mastered the art of the certainty of resolute faith. I thank You and praise You that You fulfill Your promises, are true to Your Word, and faithfully love us, enabling us to grow and cultivate a heart that never wavers in trusting in Your goodness."

Presenting the Situation

Use this portion to speak with the Lord about any areas where you've experienced doubt, fear, anxiety, or a general lack of assurance in your husband, whether in his dialogue with you or in his conversations or actions with others. Take these to God in prayer, asking Him to provide ways of confirmation that will build and strengthen your husband's faith and certainty regarding these specific situations. Affirm your trust in Christ's shed blood as full payment of your eternal salvation. If you or your husband is going through a sustained difficult period, guard against doubting the kindness and goodness of the Lord. Remember that God works everything for your ultimate good and His shining glory!

Praying for Blessing and Intervention

Gracious Lord, give my husband an unwavering belief in You, Your Word, Your promises, and Your character. Help Him to be able to discern Your leading so he can rest in the certainty of knowing he is walking in obedience to You. For those times when You withhold clarity to deepen our faith in you, I ask that we will not waver or lose trust. I ask that You send him small victories of his faith so he gains even more faith in You. Let these experiences build upon each other, and help him to remember the victories You have sent him. Surround him with men of certainty who will model strong confidence in You. Help me to honor my husband's faith by refraining from doubt, questions, and even a dismissive heart. Strengthen my own certainty in Your truth as well, Lord, so that I can join him equally on our lifelong journey of faith. In Christ's name, amen.

42

Commitment: Enriching Our Sexuality

"How beautiful you are and how pleasing, my love, with your delights!" (Song of Solomon 7:6).

Praising God

Heavenly Father, one of the greatest gifts You have given to us in our marriage is the gift of our sexuality and physical intimacy with each other. You have instructed each husband to 'enjoy life with your wife, whom you love' (Ecclesiastes 9:9). I praise You for creating this uniquely remarkable form of expressing love, pleasure, and communication with each other. As You tell us in Song of Solomon 7:6-13, our sexual relationship is to be deep, passionate, and powerful: '[The Husband:] How beautiful you are and how pleasing, my love, with your delights! Your stature is like that of the palm, and your breasts like clusters of fruit. I said, "I will climb the palm tree; I will take hold of its fruit." May your breasts be like clusters of grapes on the vine, the fragrance of your breath like apples, and your mouth like the best wine. [The Wife:] May the wine go straight to my beloved, flowing gently over lips and teeth. I belong to my beloved, and his desire is for me. Come, my beloved, let us go to the countryside, let us spend the night in the villages. Let us go early to the vineyards to see if the vines have budded, if their blossoms have opened, and if the pomegranates are in bloom—there I will give you my love. The mandrakes send out their fragrance, and at our door is every delicacy, both new and old, that I have stored up for you, my beloved.'"

Presenting the Situation

Use this portion to thank God for the areas of your physical intimacy with your husband that bring you and him great pleasure and deepen your relationship. Ask God to heal anything in your spirit or in his that has been brought about by illicit or immoral sexual experiences, including any type of pornography. Affirm your obedience to the Lord that you will not withhold sex according to His commandment in 1 Corinthians 7:3,5: "Let the husband render to his wife the affection due her, and likewise also the wife to her husband...Do not deprive one another except with consent for a time, that you may give yourselves to fasting and prayer; and come together again so that Satan does not tempt you because of your lack of self-control" (NKJV). Thank God that it is His will that your sexual relationship within marriage is beautiful, enthralling, entertaining, and fulfilling to the both of you.

Praying for Blessing and Intervention

Gracious Lord, increase the physical attraction and appetite that my husband and I have toward each other. Light the fires of passion and draw us close to each other in mutually satisfying ways. Show us the depths of pleasure and closeness through sexuality that we have not yet reached, even if we have a truly satisfying relationship. I believe that You can make it even better. Give us both grace to obey You and not withhold sex from each other, especially when we are not getting along very well. Give us wisdom on how to make food, work, and time-commitment choices that will maintain optimal levels of energy and mental clarity so that we can fully engage in this marital gift. In Christ's name, amen.

43

Communion:
Clarity on Direction

*"He refreshes my soul. He guides me along the
right paths for his name's sake"* (Psalm 23:3).

Praising God

Heavenly Father, Psalm 119:130 tells us, 'The unfolding of your words gives light; it gives understanding to the simple.' Your Word is a revealer of guidance, wisdom, and truth. When we lack clarity of direction, You make it clear through an abiding connection with You. I praise You for providing us with the ability to tap into Your light through meditation and reflection on Your Word. So much time and energy are wasted running after that which is not from You. Thank You for providing the pathway to seeking true enlightenment and guidance whenever we need it as a couple and whenever my husband needs it regarding his relationships, desires, work, and all else."

Presenting the Situation

Use this portion to explore areas in your husband's life where he may be needing additional direction and guidance. Engage in conversation with the Lord concerning these areas and ask

Him to reveal to you any areas you are unaware of. When you notice your husband is troubled, ask him to share what is going on in his life and then bring it before the Lord. Speak to God about the need for the full manifestation of His direction for your husband in these areas, and inquire of anything you can do to help be a part of that process.

Praying for Blessing and Intervention

> Gracious Lord, reveal to my husband Your direction for his life. Give clarity on the large things like his work, his ambitions and volunteer service, and our family. But also give clarity on the everyday things, like how he spends time in the evenings or on the weekends, and how we spend time together. Guide him onto the path that will bring about the full revelation of the dreams You've planted within his spirit to fulfill. Show him what it is You've created him to live out as his destiny. Help me to be supportive when he discusses these topics with me. Grant him guidance on the dreams You've created me to live out, particularly as his wife, so that he can also support and embrace Your purpose in my life. In Christ's name, amen.

44

Communication: Supporting My Growth and Purpose

*"Encourage one another and build each other up, just
as in fact you are doing"* (1 Thessalonians 5:11).

Praising God

Heavenly Father, I praise You because You have destined me
to live out the dream and purpose You've placed within me.
You have a plan for me, and it is a good plan, filled with both
a future and a hope (Jeremiah 29:11). Thank You for weaving
together my personality, skills, and passions to intersect into the
dreams You are wishing me to live out. I know these dreams—
those good works that You particularly prepared for me—will
bring You glory and they will bring other people good. Thank
You for pairing me with my husband in Your infinite wisdom,
knowing that he is an intricate part of You bringing about the
fullness of the purpose You have for me."

Presenting the Situation

Use this portion to talk with God about specific interests,
passions, and dreams of yours that you feel you are not yet fulfilling. Thank Him for the things that you have done that fully

express who you are in Him and who He has created you to be. Ask Him to enlighten you about the things He has planned for you as a part of His overarching destiny. And talk to Him about ways you'd like to see your husband more engaged and more supportive in your pursuit of your dreams both within and without your marriage.

Praying for Blessing and Intervention

> Gracious Lord, please help my husband to embrace the roles and dreams You've created me to live out. Help him not to feel like they are a competition to the love I have for him. Rather, help him to take joy in witnessing me use my gifts, skills, and passion to further the Lord's will on earth and bring Him glory. Help me to be able to share with my husband about the successes You allow me to have in such a way that he is eager to support and encourage me to do more. I also pray that whatever I do, it will be secondary to the commitment I have to our marriage and family. Please lead my husband to rest in this assurance, thus enabling him to support me all the more. Please bless my husband in his efforts to edify and support me in serving You. In Christ's name, amen.

45

Community:
Encouraging Other Couples

"Let us consider how we may spur one another on
toward love and good deeds" (Hebrews 10:24).

Praising God

Heavenly Father, You instruct us in Philippians 2:4 that we are not to only look at our own interests but also to the interests of others. We are to influence and inspire others in their marriages, and in life in general. Please bring younger couples needing encouragement into our lives so we can mentor them. Please lead an older and more mature couple to walk alongside us and guide us in our marital journey. I praise You that You enable us to encourage other couples by sharing how prayer is so powerful in impacting our marriage. You are never only about one person but You look at us as Your whole family, and therefore as I grow and develop more deeply in prayer for my husband, I ask that You expand the borders of my influence to give me the opportunity to bring many more wives to a place of prayer and support for their husbands as well."

Presenting the Situation

Use this portion to ask God to bring to your mind specific

people you know whom you can help disciple in the area of praying for their husband and also for their marriage and family. Ask the Lord to increase your confidence in being used by Him to help others grow in this area. Pray that God opens new doors of opportunity where you can engage in conversations with wives about the power of praying for their husbands. Think through ways you can honor both his and your parents in your marriage. Ask them to share the lessons they have learned with you so you can grow in wisdom from their victories and mistakes.

Praying for Blessing and Intervention

> Gracious Lord, I surrender myself to be used by You and ask that You bring people along my path with whom I can share about the power of praying for my husband, myself, and our marriage. Give me winsomeness and charisma and give our marriage a glow so that others will inquire about what we do. I ask that You open and prepare hearts toward the ministry of committed prayer for their marriage and that You will glorify Yourself through the process of drawing more and more couples to You to be used by You to encourage an even greater number of others. In Christ's name, amen.

46

Communication: Talking with Each Other

*"My dear brothers and sisters, take note of this:
Everyone should be quick to listen, slow to speak
and slow to become angry"* (James 1:19).

Praising God

Heavenly Father, relationships are one of the most important things You have given to us to experience while on earth. And the marriage relationship is especially important, valuable, and purposeful. I praise You for creating us as relational beings who can benefit from each other and build into each other. Thank You for the ability to communicate, whether it's through words, touch, texts, or a myriad of other ways. I praise You for the desire You have placed within us to connect with others on a meaningful level, and I ask that You increase that desire more in the days, weeks, months, and years ahead."

Presenting the Situation

Use this portion to thank God for the blessing He has already given you and your husband in this area of communication. Focus on what has worked and why it has worked so well. Let God hear your appreciation for each of these things. Spend some time bringing to the Lord the aspects of your communication with your spouse that contain an element of struggle and misunderstanding. Invite Him to intervene in these specific places, providing you both with a greater clarity of thought, a respect for each other, and an ability to perceive what the other person is really communicating. Ask Him to give you both a gentle spirit toward each other, particularly related to the areas of communication that are challenging.

Praying for Blessing and Intervention

Gracious Lord, help my husband and me both to be quick to hear, slow to speak, and slow to anger when we communicate with each other (James 1:19). Help us always to lead with love and to give the benefit of the doubt in our understanding of what the other is seeking to communicate. Give us a relationship that is conducive to being open, honest, and authentic with each other. Help us in our busy schedules to cultivate regular periods of time where we communicate as a couple. Give me courage to discuss those troubling areas in my life and marriage and not withdraw in silent or hidden frustration. Help me to speak about these areas to my husband in love with open honesty. Grant my husband an open and receptive heart without anger or defensiveness. Please also add an element of greater spontaneity and fun into our communication. Let us flirt with each other more in what we say and how we say it, and revive in us a spirit of playfulness and cheer. In Christ's name, amen.

47

Commitment: Physical Health

*"Dear friend, I pray that you may enjoy good
health and that all may go well with you, even
as your soul is getting along well"* (3 John 2).

Praising God

Heavenly Father, our bodies are Your temple and You've given them to us to serve and honor You while always edifying and encouraging others. Over time and with busy schedules, it's easy to let our physical appearance, fitness, and health slide. Yet I praise You that You have reminded us in Your Word that we have been bought with a price and are to glorify You with our bodies (1 Corinthians 6:20). I praise You for instructing and guiding us in the way we should go. You have given us so many insights into what is necessary for maintaining optimal physical health, well-being, and attractiveness so that each of us in our marriage benefit fully from the other."

Presenting the Situation

Use this portion to bring up anything to God where you feel that your husband needs to focus regarding his physical health, fitness, and overall well-being. This includes his diet and the amount of sleep he gets each night. It also includes his personal hygiene or exercise. Wherever you believe that the Lord could help motivate your husband toward greater physical well-being, ask Him to do so. Also talk to God about any areas of your own physical well-being where you would want His assistance in helping you improve.

Praying for Blessing and Intervention

Gracious Lord, I ask for Your blessing on my husband's physical body. I ask that You maintain his health and invigorate him with strength. Motivate him to make healthy eating choices that will bring benefit to his body. Help me to encourage him in these choices through my own healthy eating, cooking, and shopping. I ask that you increase the desire in both of us to be physically fit and strengthen our bodies through regular exercise. Help us to keep our bodies active and to present our bodies to each other in such a way that evokes attraction and desire. In Christ's name, amen.

48

Commitment:
Fun and Enjoyment

"Enjoy life with your wife, whom you love, all the
days of this meaningless life that God has given
you under the sun—all your meaningless days.
For this is your lot in life and in your toilsome
labor under the sun" (Ecclesiastes 9:9).

Praising God

Heavenly Father, You have created us in such a way that we take pleasure from many things in our lives. Within each of us is a desire for fun, enjoyment, and adventure. Living in a marriage and having a family—on top of work, life responsibilities, and all else—can sometimes shift our focus from what we enjoy onto what we must do to move on to the next day. While responsibility, diligence, and hard work are good, God, so are enjoyment and a spirit of fun. I praise You for creating so much in Your great world that provides us with wonderful things to taste, see, experience, explore, and enjoy. I praise You for planting within us a seed of discovery and pleasure. Let that grow and maintain itself in our marriage so that each day is fresh and each moment contains an element of mystery and delight."

Presenting the Situation

Use this portion to thank God for the times you and your husband have genuinely experienced pleasure and fun together. Reminisce on vacations you've taken together and the events you've attended together. It could be your regular time together that surfaces warm memories and thoughts of fun, or just staying home and watching a movie. Whatever it is, take this moment to thank God for all these meaningful times together. Then bring up to the Lord those areas in your life where fun and playfulness may have gone missing, and ask Him to spark delight in the both of you once again, for each other and for life itself.

Praying for Blessing and Intervention

Gracious Lord, bless us with an abundance of joy and fun in our marriage relationship. Whether it's as simple as a stroll in the park or as lavish as a cruise or an overseas vacation, it doesn't matter to me so much what it is but rather that my husband and I maintain an element of excitement in all that we do for fun together. Give my husband a creative spirit to explore things we've never done before. Reveal to us ways that we can ignite the flames of fun in our conversations and even in the many duties that must be carried out simply as part of living. Delight us with Your love, and in Your love, delight us with each other. Remind us to have fun, my God, and make enjoying each other a priority. In Christ's name, amen.

49

Character: Mutual Respect and Honor

"Do nothing out of selfish ambition or vain conceit. Rather, in humility value others above yourselves" (Philippians 2:3).

Praising God

Heavenly Father, respect and honor are building blocks in the foundation of any marriage relationship. Without these, the laws of love, like kindness, mercy, trust, and grace, go out the window. I praise You, Jesus, that You operate in the realm of both respect and honor and have modeled for us what these qualities look like, even in the face of Your persecution, rejection, and betrayal. You are the hallmark of these two qualities, and I thank You for living with me in an understanding way when I fail to give You or my husband one or the other. I praise You that Your Word instructs us in the path of love and highlights this as the ultimate covering for all relational issues, disappointments, and challenges."

Presenting the Situation

Use this portion to ask God to forgive you for any time you have failed to speak or act with respect or honor toward your husband. Bring up specific things that you remember so that you can address them directly with God and, if necessary, with your husband. Ask God to give you a spirit of forgiveness and to remove the spirit of bitterness with regard to any of the times your husband has failed to treat you with respect or honor. Seek the Lord's provision of both traits in the various areas of your marriage where you may feel they are lacking most, whether in your conversations, actions, decision-making processes, money-spending habits, physical intimacy, or any other.

Praying for Blessing and Intervention

> Gracious Lord, please give my husband and me the blessing of living in a marriage that is highlighted with both respect and honor. Bless us with this gift from You in a way that comes naturally to us. Pour out Your lovingkindness on each of us so that it overflows to the other. Where there has been disrespect, let the other respond with gentleness and grace. Where there has been dishonor, let the other respond with peace and patience. May our responses to each other be punctuated with the spirit of love so that we habitually operate wholly and completely in an atmosphere that knows nothing other than respect and honor. In Christ's name, amen.

50

Commitment: Accepting and Embracing Each Other

"Do not judge, and you will not be judged. Do not condemn, and you will not be condemned. Forgive, and you will be forgiven" (Luke 6:37).

Praising God

Heavenly Father, criticism, judgment, and unrealistic expectations destroy the union of intimacy and hinder Your plan in our marriage relationship. I praise You for accepting and embracing me, despite my multiple faults, sins, and imperfections. You are the perfect example of what true acceptance and embracing means. I praise You for the way You make me feel fully loved, cherished, and adored. And I thank You that You call my husband and me to love, accept, and embrace each other in this capacity as well."

Presenting the Situation

Use this portion to ask God to open your heart to accept and embrace the things about your husband that are not "sins" but are things you may not naturally accept and embrace. It could be something he does that annoys you or even things about how he looks or interacts with you. Thank God for the times and experiences in your life where you have felt truly accepted, cherished, and embraced by your spouse and ask God to provide ways for you to demonstrate the same level of authentic love to him.

Praying for Blessing and Intervention

Gracious Lord, help me to love my husband from a pure heart so that he will truly be blessed by my acceptance and embracing of him. Please diminish in my own mind and perception those things in his life that make me uncomfortable or less than satisfied. Draw my attention to his qualities that make me so easily feel a heart of love and attraction for him. Help me to focus on those qualities and to build him up through my love and acceptance. I pray the same for him toward me. I ask that You will guide our hearts and communication with such grace that we encourage the changes in our lives that the other desires in us. Grant to both of us the ability to be open to the preferences of our spouse and to receive them with openness and acceptance. Guide us to change our attitudes and behaviors so that they become ever increasingly a pleasure to our spouse. In Christ's name, amen.

WANT A TASTE OF WHAT IT MEANS TO DREAM AGAIN?

Join Bruce Wilkinson for this life-changing 12-week course and learn the strategies to re-engage with your passions and truly live your dream.

Unlock your dream through exclusive access to this online, self-paced course offering:

- Brand NEW weekly video lessons from Bruce
- Course content
- Personal study & reflection
- A pathway to pursue your dreams!

Discover the future you've only dreamed of before!

DREAM AGAIN

12-WEEK COURSE

BRUCE WILKINSON

BruceWilkinson.com

To learn more about Harvest House books and
to read sample chapters, visit our website:

www.harvesthousepublishers.com

HARVEST HOUSE PUBLISHERS
EUGENE, OREGON